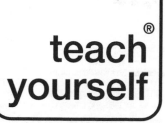

instant russian
elisabeth smith

D0658100

For over 60 years, more than
50 million people have learnt over
750 subjects the **teach yourself**
way, with impressive results.

be where you want to be
with **teach yourself**

30130 142343697

Essex County Council Libraries

For UK order enquiries: please contact Bookpoint Ltd, 130 Milton Park, Abingdon, Oxon, OX14 4SB. Telephone: +44 (0) 1235 827720. Fax: +44 (0) 1235 400454. Lines are open 09.00–17.00, Monday to Saturday, with a 24-hour message answering service. Details about our titles and how to order are available at www.teachyourself.co.uk

For USA order enquiries: please contact McGraw-Hill Customer Services, PO Box 545, Blacklick, OH 43004-0545, USA. Telephone: 1-800-722-4726. Fax: 1-614-755-5645.

For Canada order enquiries: please contact McGraw-Hill Ryerson Ltd, 300 Water St, Whitby, Ontario. L1N 9B6, Canada. Telephone: 905 430 5000. Fax: 905 430 5020.

Long renowned as the authoritative source for self-guided learning – with more than 50 million copies sold worldwide – the **teach yourself** series includes over 500 titles in the fields of languages, crafts, hobbies, business, computing and education.

British Library Cataloguing in Publication Data: a catalogue record for this title is available from the British Library.

Library of Congress Catalog Card Number: on file.

First published in UK 2000 by Hodder Education, 338 Euston Road, London, NW1 3BH.

First published in US 2000 by The McGraw-Hill Companies, Inc.

This edition published 2006.

The **teach yourself** name is a registered trade mark of Hodder Headline.

Typeset by Transet Limited, Coventry, England.
Printed in Great Britain for Hodder Education, a division of Hodder Headline, 338 Euston Road, London, NW1 3BH, by Cox & Wyman Ltd, Reading, Berkshire.

The publisher has used its best endeavours to ensure that the URLs for external websites referred to in this book are correct and active at the time of going to press. However, the publisher and the author have no responsibility for the websites and can make no guarantee that a site will remain live or that the content will remain relevant, decent or appropriate.

Hodder Headline's policy is to use papers that are natural, renewable and recyclable products and made from wood grown in sustainable forests. The logging and manufacturing processes are expected to conform to the environmental regulations of the country of origin.

Impression number   10 9 8 7 6 5 4 3 2 1
Year   2010 2009 2008 2007 2006

contents

read this first		5
how this book works		7
progress chart		9
week 1	**day-by-day guide**	11
	f samalyotee – new words – pronunciation – good news grammar – learn by heart – let's speak Russian – test your progress	
week 2	**day-by-day guide**	25
	f Sankt-Peeteeboorgee – new words – good news grammar – let's speak Russian – learn by heart – test your progress	
week 3	**day-by-day guide**	37
	mi dyelaeem pakoopkee – new words – spot the keys – good news grammar – learn by heart – let's speak Russian – test your progress	
week 4	**day-by-day guide**	49
	mi eedyom v reestaran – new words – good news grammar – learn by heart – spot the keys – say it simply – let's speak Russian – test your progress	
week 5	**day-by-day guide**	63
	f pootee – new words – learn by heart – good news grammar – let's speak Russian – spot the keys – test your progress	

4

contents

week 6   **day-by-day guide**   **75**
f aerapartoo – new words – learn by heart –
good news grammar – spot the keys –
say it simply – let's speak Russian –
test your progress

answers   **86**
flash cards   **92**
certificate   **127**

read this first

If, like me, you usually skip introductions, don't! Read on! You need to know how **Instant Russian** works and why.

When I decided to write the **Instant** series I first called it *Barebones*, because that's what you want: *no frills, no fuss, just the bare bones and go!* So in **Instant Russian** you'll find:

- Only 461 words to say everything, well... nearly everything.

- No ghastly grammar – just a few useful tips.

- No time wasters such as 'the pen of my aunt...'

- No phrase book phrases for vodka sampling sessions in Siberia.

- No need to struggle with the Russian script – everything is in easy phonetic language.

- No need to be perfect. Mistakes won't spoil your success.

I've put some 30 years of teaching experience into this course. I know how people learn. I also know for how long they are motivated by a new project (a few weeks) and how little time they can spare to study each day (under an hour). That's why you'll complete **Instant Russian** in six weeks and get away with 45 minutes a day.

Of course there is some learning to do, but I have tried to make it as much fun as possible, even when it is boring. You'll meet Tom and Kate Walker on holiday in Russia. They do the kind of things you need to know about: shopping, eating out and getting about. As you will note, Tom and Kate speak **Instant Russian** all the time, even to each other. What paragons of virtue!

To get the most out of this course, there are only two things you really should do:

- Follow the **Day-by-day guide** as suggested. Please don't skip bits and short-change your success. Everything is there for a reason.
- If you are a complete beginner, buy the recording that accompanies this book. It will help you to speak faster and with confidence.

When you have filled in your **Certificate** at the end of the book and can speak **Instant Russian**, I would like to hear from you. Why not visit my website www.elisabeth-smith.co.uk, e-mail me at elisabeth.smith@hodder.co.uk, or write to me care of Hodder Education, 338 Euston Road, London, NW1 3BH?

Elisabeth Smith

The author would like to thank Rachel Farmer and Alexandra Borodulina, who acted as language consultants in the preparation of this book.

how this book works

Instant Russian has been structured for your rapid success. This is how it works:

Day-by-day guide Stick to it. If you miss a day, add one.

Dialogues Follow Tom and Kate through Russia. The English is in 'Russian-speak' to get you tuned in.

New words Don't fight them, don't skip them – learn them! The flash cards will help you.

Good news grammar After you read it you can forget half and still succeed! That's why it's good news.

Flash words and flash sentences Read about these building blocks in the flash card section on page 92. Then use them!

Learn by heart Obligatory! Memorizing puts you on the fast track to speaking in full sentences.

Let's speak Russian *You* will be doing the talking – in Russian. Best with the recording.

Spot the keys Listen to rapid Russian and make sense of it.

Say it simply Learn how to use plain, **Instant Russian** to say what you want to say. Don't be shy!

Test your progress Mark your own test and be amazed by the result.

Answers This is where you'll find the answers to the exercises.

▶ This icon asks you to switch on the recording.

Pronunciation If you don't know about it and don't have the recording go straight to page 15. You need to know about pronunciation before you can start Week 1.

Progress chart Enter your score each week and monitor your progress. Are you going for *very good* or *outstanding*?

Certificate It's on the last page. In six weeks it will have your name on it!

progress chart

At the end of each week record your test score on the Progress chart below.

At the end of the course throw out your worst result – anybody can have a bad week – and add up your *five* best weekly scores. Divide the total by five to get your average score and overall course result.

Write your result – *outstanding, excellent, very good* or *good* – on your **Certificate** at the end of the book. If you scored more than 80% enlarge it and frame it!

Progress chart

90–100%							outstanding
80–89%							excellent
70–79%							very good
60–69%							good
Weeks	1	2	3	4	5	6	

Total of five best weeks =

divided by five =

Your final result _____ %

01

week one

Study for 45 minutes – or a little longer if you can!

Day zero

- Open the book and read **Read this first.**
- Now read **How this book works**.

Day one

- Read **In the aeroplane**.
- Listen to/Read **F samalyotee**.
- Listen to/Read the **New words**, then learn some of them.

Day two

- Repeat **F samalyotee** and the **New words**.
- Listen to/Read **Pronunciation**.
- Learn more **New words**.

Day three

- Learn all the **New words** until you know them well.
- Use the **Flash words** to help you.
- Read and learn the **Good news grammar**.

Day four

- Cut out and learn the **Flash sentences**.
- Listen to/Read **Learn by heart**.

Day five

- Listen to/Read **Let's speak Russian**.
- Revise! Tomorrow you'll be testing your progress.

Day six

- Listen to/Read **Let's speak more Russian** (optional).
- Listen to/Read **Let's speak Russian – fast and fluently** (optional).
- Translate **Test your progress**.

Day seven is your day off!

day-by-day guide

In the aeroplane

Tom and Kate Walker are on their way to Russia. They are boarding flight SU 254 to Yalta via Moscow and squeeze past Yuriy Zhivago who is sitting in their row. (The English is in 'Russian-speak' to get you tuned in.)

Tom	Excuse me, please, by us (we have) seats 9a and 9b.
Yuriy	Yes?... little minute (just a moment), please.
Tom	Hello. We – Tom and Kate Walker.
Yuriy	Hello. Me they call (I am called) Zhivago.
Tom	Dr Zhivago?
Yuriy	No, unfortunately. I – Yuriy Zhivago.
Tom	We are going to Yalta. You also?
Yuriy	No, I am going to Moscow. But I from Novgorod.
Tom	Novgorod very beautiful town. I was there in May, on business.
Yuriy	Who you? (What do you do?)
Tom	I programmer. Computers. I work at Unilever.
Yuriy	And you, Mrs Walker? Who you? Where do you work?
Kate	I worked in travel agency. Now I work in Rover. The work there better.
Yuriy	You from London?
Kate	No, we from Manchester. We were three years in London and a year in New York. Now we in Birmingham.
Yuriy	I worked in the university. Now I work in bank.
Kate	Work in bank good?
Yuriy	Work boring. But money (of money) more. By me (I have) big flat, Mercedes, wife, son and daughter. My wife from America. By her (she has) parents in Los Angeles and girlfriend in Florida. She always rings to them. It (is) costs expensive.
Kate	We now in holiday (on holiday). You also?
Yuriy	No, unfortunately. By me (I have) in August holiday. We are going to Greece. By us (we have) there house... summer home – without telephone. And we go there without mobile phone!

▶ F samalyotee

Tom and Kate Walker are on their way to Russia. They are boarding flight SU 254 to Yalta via Moscow and squeeze past Yuriy Zhivago who is sitting in their row.

Tom	Eezveeneetee, pazhaloosta, oo nas meesta 9a ee 9b.
Yuriy	Da?... meenootachkoo, pazhaloosta.
Tom	Zdrastvooiytee. Mi – Tom ee Kate Walker.
Yuriy	Zdrastvooiytee. Meenya zavoot Zhivaga.
Tom	Doktar Zhivaga?
Yuriy	Nyet, k sazhilyeneeyu. Ya – Yuriy Zhivaga.
Tom	Mi yedeem v Yaltoo. Vi tozhe?
Yuriy	Nyet. Ya yedoo v Maskvoo. No ya eez Novgarada.
Tom	Novgarat ocheen' kraseeviiy gorat. Ya tam bil v maee, pa beeznisoo.
Yuriy	Kto vi?
Tom	Ya pragrameest. Kamp'yutiri. Ya rabotayu v Ooneeleeveerye.
Yuriy	A vi, meesees Walker? Kto vi? Gdee vi rabotaeetee?
Kate	Ya rabotala v tooragyentstvee. Seechyas ya rabotayu v Roveerye. Rabota tam loochshe.
Yuriy	Vi eez Londana?
Kate	Nyet. Mi eez Manchyes'teera. Mi bilee tree goda v Londanee ee got v Nyu Yorkee. Seechyas mi v Beermeengyemee.
Yuriy	Ya rabotal v ooneeveerseetyetee. Seechyas ya rabotayu v bankee.
Kate	Rabota v bankee kharoshaya?
Yuriy	Rabota skoochnaya. No dyeneek bol'shi. Oo meenya bal'shaya kvarteera, Meerseedes, zhina, sin ee doch. Maya zhina eez Amyereekee. Oo neeyo radeeteeli v Los Anzhileesee ee padrooga v Flareedee. Ana vseegda zvaneet eem. Eta stoeet doraga.
Kate	Mi seechyas v otpooskee. Vi tozhe?
Yuriy	Nyet, k sazhilyeneeyu. Oo meenya v avgoostee otpoosk. Mi yedeem v Gryetsiyu. Oo nas tam dom... dachya – bees teeleefona. Mi yedeem tooda bees sotavava!

▶ New words

Learning words the traditional way can be boring. If you enjoy the **Flash cards** why not make your own for the rest of the words? Always say the words OUT LOUD. It's the fast track to speaking!

v, va, f   *in, to, at*
sama**lyot**(ee)   *aeroplane*
eezveen**ee**tee   *excuse me*
pazh**a**loosta   *please*
oo nas   *by us (we have)*
m**ee**sta   *places, seats*
a... b   a... b (pronounced ah... *bay*)
ee   *and*
da   *yes*
meen**oo**tachkoo   *little minute*
zd**ra**stvooiytee   *hello*
mi   *we*
meen**ya** zav**oo**t   *they call me (I am called)*
nyet   *no*
k sazhil**ye**neeyu   *unfortunately*
ya   *I*
yedeem   *we go (travel)*
yedoo   *I go (travel)*
vi   *you (polite)*
t**o**zhe   *also*
no   *but*
eez, ees   *from*
ocheen'   *very*
kras**ee**viiy   *beautiful*
g**o**rad, g**o**rat   *town*
tam   *there*
bil   *was*
b**i**lee   *were*
v m**a**ee   *in May*
dlya   *for*
pa be**ez**nisoo   *on business*
kto   *who*
rab**o**tayu   *I work*
rab**o**taeetee   *you work*
pragram**ee**st   *computer programmer*

kamp'**yu**tir/kamp'**yu**tiri   *computer*
gdye   *where*
rab**o**tala   *I, she worked*
rab**o**tal   *I, he worked*
v toorag**ye**ntstvee   *in a/the travel agency*
seech**ya**s   *now*
rab**o**ta   *work, job*
l**oo**chshe   *better*
tree   *three*
g**o**da/got   *year*
v ooneeveerseet**ye**tee   *at a/the university*
bank/v b**a**nkee   *bank/in, at bank*
khar**o**chaya   *good*
sk**oo**chnaya   *boring*
d**ye**neek   *money*
b**o**l'shi   *more*
oo meen**ya**   *I have*
bal'sh**a**ya   *big*
kvart**e**era   *flat*
m**a**ya, moiy   *my*
zh**i**na   *wife*
sin   *son*
doch   *daughter*
oo nee**yo**   *she has*
rad**ee**teelee   *parents*
padr**oo**ga   *girlfriend*
an**a**   *she*
vse**e**gda   *always*
zvan**ee**t   *rings, phones*
eem   *to them*
eta   *it is*
st**o**eet   *costs*
d**o**raga   *expensive*
v **o**tpooskee   *on holiday*
v **av**goos'tee   *in August*

tam *there*
dom *house*
dachya *summer house*

bees teeleefona *without
    telephone*
sotaviy (teeleefon) *mobile
    telephone*

**TOTAL NEW WORDS: 75
...only 306 words to go!**

Some easy extras

Myeseetsi (months)

yanvar', feevral', mart, apryel', maiy, eeyun', eeyul', avgoost,
seentyabr', aktyabr', nayabr', deekabr'

Tsifri (numerals)

adeen *1*		shes't' *6*	
dva *2*		syem' *7*	
tree *3*		voseem' *8*	
cheetiree *4*		dyeveet' *9*	
pyat' *5*		dyeseet' *10*	

More greetings

dobraye ootra *good morning*, dobriiy dyen' *good day, good afternoon*;
dobriiy vyecheer *good evening*; da sveedaneeya *goodbye*

▶ Pronunciation

The Russian language is beautiful, so drop all inhibitions and
try to speak Russian rather than English with the words
changed. If Russian pronunciation is new to you, please buy the
recording and listen to the real thing.

As you can see, all the words in **Instant Russian** have been
transliterated into phonetic language. That makes it much
easier, especially if you are in a hurry. You don't have to learn
the Cyrillic alphabet first but can start speaking straight away.

The guide to vowels and consonants will get you started.
Sometimes it takes a lot of English letters – for example *shsh* –
to produce the sound of one Russian letter, but you'll soon pick
it up.

Vowels

Say the sound OUT LOUD and then the Russian example OUT LOUD.

a	like *a* in *father*	bal'shaya
e	like *e* in *let*	eta
ee	like *ee* in *feet*	eezveeneetee
i	like *i* in *still*	mi
iy	like *y* in *boy*	kraseeviiy
o	like *o* in *bore*	Londan
oo	like *oo* in *shoot*	loochshee

y plus vowel

ya	like *ya* in *yard*	ya
ye	like *ye* in *yet*	nyet
yo	like *yo* in *yonder*	oo neeyo
yu	like *u* in *universal*	ya rabotayu

Consonants

g	is always pronounced as a 'hard' *g*, as in *goat*	
r	is rolled (as in Italian)	
v	like *v* in *vase*	
zh	like *s* in *pleasure*	tozhe
kh	like *ch* in *loch*	kharoshaya
ts	like *ts* in *quits*	tsar
sh	like *sh* in *shout*	shes't'
shsh	like *sh sh* in *posh ship*	eeshshyo
l', t'		skol'ka
iy	like *y* in *toy*	maiy

When you see a ' after a letter try to slip in a very soft *y*.

Accent

The letter in **bold** tells you to stress the syllable in which it appears. Example: Maskvoo, rabotayu. The stress is especially important when you come across the vowel o. If it is stressed, it is pronounced like the o in *bore*; if it is not stressed, it is pronounced like the a in *sofa*.

When you go to Russia you'll want to know a little of the Cyrillic script, too. So, as an introduction here's the Russian alphabet. And later in the course there'll also be a few useful flash words in 'real' Russian script, to help you on your way.

А Б В Г Д Е Ё Ж З И Й К Л М Н О П Р
а б в г д е ё ж з и й к л м н о п р

С Т У Ф Х Ц Ч Ш Щ Ъ Ы Ь Э Ю Я
с т у ф х ц ч ш щ ъ ы ь э ю я

▶ Good news grammar

This is the good news part of each week. Remember I promised *no ghastly grammar*! I simply explain the differences between Russian and English. This will help you to speak Russian **Instantly!**

1 Words for 'the' and 'a'

There aren't any! So 'bank' in Russian means either *a bank* or *the bank* and the plural 'bankee' means either *some banks* or *the banks*.

2 The Russian words for 'am', 'are', 'is'

There aren't any! So all you need to say in Russian is:

I computer programmer = Ya pragrameest

3 The Russian words for 'have', 'has'

There aren't any! Russian uses a different sort of phrase and says, literally, *by me (there is)* = Oo meenya.

Example: *I have a flat* = Oo meenya kvarteera.

Here is the complete list. Spend ten minutes on it until you know it with your eyes closed.

oo meen**ya**	*I have*
oo vas	*you have*
oo neev**o**, oo nee**yo**	*he has, she has*
oo nas	*we have*
oo neekh	*they have*

4 Saying 'you'

Russian has two words for *you*. If you know one person well, or are speaking to a child, use 'ti'; if you are being polite and formal to one person use 'vi' or if you are speaking to more than one person, also use 'vi'. In **Instant Russian** you only use 'vi'.

5 Doing things

Did you notice that when you say *I*, *we* or *you* in Russian the ending of the verb changes? Here are the verbs you came across in the dialogue. Have another look at them. They are not for learning. You have done that already.

rabotat' *to work*		yekhat' *to travel*	
ya rabotayu	*I work*	ya yedoo	*I travel*
mi rabotaeem	*we work*	mi yedeem	*we travel*
vi rabotaeetee	*you work*	vi yedeetee	*you travel*

6 *V*: in, at, to

As you saw in the **New words** the Russian letter 'v' (va)/'f' can mean *in, at, to* and sometimes even *on*, as in *on holiday* – 'v otpooskee'. That's the easy bit. Unfortunately, after a 'v' the ending of the following word changes. So 'Maskva' becomes 'Maskvoo' (*to Moscow*) and 'bank' becomes 'bankye' (*at the bank*). But don't worry about it. This is just for knowing, not for learning! You'll pick it up as you go along.

7 Asking questions

Vi tozhe. *You, too.* Vi tozhe? *You, too?* You simply use your voice to turn a statement into a question. Easy!

▶ Learn by heart

Don't be tempted to skip this exercise because it reminds you of school... If you want to speak, not stumble, saying a few lines by heart does the trick!

Learn 'Meenya zavoot' by heart after you have filled in the gaps with your personal, or any, information.

> **Example**: Meenya zavoot Colin Bell.
> Ya eez Londana.

When you know the seven lines by heart, go over them again until you can say them out loud fluently and fairly fast. Can you beat 40 seconds?

Meenya zavoot

Meenya zavoot ....(NAME)
Ya eez ....(PLACE)
Ya rabotayu v bankee ....
Oo meenya bal'shaya kvarteera. Ana doroga stoeet.
V martee ya bil/bila v ....(PLACE)
F seenteebrye mi yedeem v ....(PLACE)
Vi tozhe?

▶ Let's speak Russian

I shall give you ten English sentences and you'll put them into Russian. Always speak OUT LOUD. After each one check the answer at the bottom of the page. Tick it if you got it right. If you have the recording, listen to check the answers to **Let's speak Russian**.

1 I am called Tom Walker.
2 Are you from London?
3 Yes, I am from London.
4 I have a girlfriend in Florida.
5 We are going to Moscow.

6 Do you have a Mercedes?
7 No, unfortunately (not).
8 We have a house in Novgorod.
9 There is more money in the bank.
10 Is the job boring?

Well, how many did you get right? If you are not happy, do it again! Now here are some questions in Russian and you are going to answer in Russian. Answer the next five questions with 'da' and 'ya'.

11 Vi eez Manchyes'teera?
12 Oo vas dom v Londanee?
13 Vi yedeetee v Maskvoo?
14 Vi rabotaeetee bees komp'yutera?
15 Vi bilee v Breestolee pa beeznisoo?

And now answer the next five questions with 'da' and 'ya', 'mi' or 'oo nas'.

16 Vi yedeetee v Novgarat?
17 Oo vas meesta 9a ee 9b?
18 Oo vas otpoosk v apryelee?
19 Vi bilee tree goda v Londanee?
20 Oo vas seechyas bol'shi dyeneek?

Answers

1 Meenya zavoot Tom Walker.
2 Vi eez Londana?
3 Da, ya eez Londana.
4 Oo meenya padrooga v Flareedee.
5 Mi yedeem v Maskvoo.
6 Oo vas Meerseedes?
7 Nyet, k sazhilyeneeyu.
8 Oo nas dom v Novgaradee.
9 V bankee bol'shi dyeneek.
10 Rabota skoochnaya?
11 Da, ya eez Manchyes'teera.
12 Da, oo meenya dom v Londanee.

13 Da, ya yedoo v Maskvoo.
14 Da, ya rabotayu bees komp'yutera.
15 Da, ya bil/bila v Breestolee pa beeznisoo.
16 Da, ya yedoo v Novgarat.
17 Da, oo nas meesta 9a ee 9b.
18 Da, oo nas otpoosk v apryelee.
19 Da, mi bilee tree goda v Londanee.
20 Da, oo nas seechyas bol'shi dyeneek.

Well, what was your score? If you ticked all of them give yourself three gold stars!

▶ Let's speak more Russian

Here are some optional exercises. They may stretch the 45 minutes a day by 15 minutes. But the extra practice will be worth it.

And always remember: near enough is good enough!

In your own words

This exercise will teach you to express yourself freely. Use only the words you have learned so far.

Tell me in your own words that...

1 you are from Manchester
2 unfortunately your work is boring
3 you have a son and daughter
4 you work in a university
5 you have a house in Birmingham
6 you are going to Moscow
7 you have a friend in London
8 Yalta is a very beautiful town
9 you are on holiday
10 a big flat in New York is very expensive

Answers

1 Ya eez Manch**yes**'tyera.
2 K sazhil**ye**neeyu rab**o**ta sk**oo**chnaya.
3 Oo myen**ya** sin ee doch.
4 Ya rab**o**tayu v ooneevyeerseet**ye**tee.
5 Oo meen**ya** dom v Beermeeng**ye**mee.
6 Ya **ye**doo v Maskv**oo**.
7 Oo meen**ya** padr**oo**ga v L**o**ndanee.
8 Yalta **o**cheen' kras**ee**viiy g**o**rat.
9 Oo meen**ya o**tpoosk.
10 Bal'shaya kvart**ee**ra v Nyu Y**o**rke st**o**eet **o**cheen' d**o**raga.

▶ Let's speak Russian – fast and fluently

No more stuttering and stumbling! Get out the stopwatch and time yourself with this fluency practice. Some of the English is in 'Russian-speak' to help you.

Translate each section and check if it is correct. Then cover up the answers and say the three or four sentences fast!

Good morning. I am going to Moscow. You too?
No, I work in New York - in a bank. Now I am going to Yalta on business.
My wife is from Novgorod.
I have in September holiday – without telephone.

*Dobraye **oo**tra. Ya **ye**doo v Maskv**oo**. Vi t**o**zhe?*
*Nyet, ya rab**o**tayu v Nyu Y**o**rke – v bank**ee**. Seech**a**s ya **ye**doo v **Ya**ltoo pa b**ee**zniso**o**.*
*M**a**ya zhin**a** eez N**o**vgar**a**da.*
*Oo meen**ya** v seenteebr**ye o**tpoosk – bees teeleef**o**na.*

Hello. Who you?
Me they call John. I have a girlfriend, Tanya. She programmer. In bank in Moscow.
I work in university. The work there very good.

*Zdrastvo**o**iytee. Kto vi?*
*Meen**ya** zav**oo**t John. Oo meen**ya** padr**oo**ga, Tanya. Ana pragram**ee**st. V bank**ee** v Maskv**ye**.*
*Ya rab**o**tayu v ooneeveerseet**ye**tee. Rab**o**ta tam khar**o**shaya.*

I have flat in Moscow. Costs very expensive.
We were two years in Moscow. Moscow very beautiful town. Now we in London.
Excuse me, little minute (just a moment) please. My wife rings.

*Oo meen**ya** kvart**ee**ra v Maskv**ye**. St**o**eet **o**cheen' d**o**raga.*
*Mi bil**ee** dva g**o**da v Maskv**ye**. Maskv**a o**cheen' kras**ee**viiy g**o**rat. Seech**a**s mi v L**o**ndanee.*
*Eezveen**ee**tee, meen**oo**tachkoo, pazhal**oo**sta. M**a**ya zhin**a** zvan**ee**t.*

Now say all the sentences in Russian without stopping and starting. If you can do it in under one minute you are a fast and fluent winner!

But if you are not happy with your result – just try once more.

Test your progress

This is your only written exercise. You'll be amazed at how easy it is! Translate the 20 sentences without looking at the previous pages. The bits in brackets help you with the difference between English and Russian.

(Please note: write the words straight: don't alternate bold type and light to show where the word is stressed. It would take you forever!)

1 They call me (I am called) Frank Lukas.
2 Hello, we (are) Viktor and Olga.
3 I (am) also from Omsk.
4 In October I was in Moscow.
5 We were three years in America.
6 London is very expensive.
7 Excuse me, please. Where (do) you work?
8 Are you working in Manchester?
9 (Are) you Viktor Izmailov from Tomsk?
10 (The) flat in Novgorod is very big.
11 Little minute (just a moment), please, by me (I have) more money.
12 There there is (a) telephone? No, unfortunately not.
13 I (am) in Yalta without (my) son.
14 (Is) (the) company big?
15 (Is) (a) Mercedes expensive?
16 In April London (is) very beautiful.
17 By him (he has) in (the) travel agency (a) girlfriend.
18 Unfortunately (the) work (is) very boring.
19 (The) job is very good, but (a) holiday is better.
20 My daughter telephones always.

When you have finished look up the answers on page 86 and mark your work. Then enter your result on the Progress chart on page 9. If your score is higher than 80% you'll have done very well indeed!

02

week two

Forty-five minutes a day – but a little extra will step up your progress!

Day one

- Read **In Saint Petersburg**.
- Listen to/Read **f Sankt-Peeteerboorgee**.
- Listen to/Read the **New words**. Learn 20 easy ones.

Day two

- Repeat **f Sankt-Peeteerboorgee** and the **New words**.
- Go over **Pronunciation**.
- Learn the harder **New words**.
- Use the **Flash words** to help you.

Day three

- Learn all the **New words** until you know them well.
- Read and learn the **Good news grammar**.

Day four

- Cut out and learn the **Flash sentences**.
- Listen to/Read **Learn by heart**.

Day five

- Listen to/Read **Let's speak Russian**.
- Go over **Learn by heart**.

Day six

- Listen to/Read **Let's speak more Russian** (optional).
- Listen to/Read **Let's speak Russian – fast and fluently** (optional).
- Translate **Test your progress**.

Day seven is a study-free day!

day-by-day guide

In Saint Petersburg

In Saint Petersburg Tom and Kate are checking in at a hotel. They speak to Olga, the receptionist at the service desk and later to Ivan, the waiter. (The English is in 'Russian-speak' to get you tuned in.)

Kate Good day. By you (do you have) room for two, for one night? Costs not too expensive?

Olga Yes, by us (we have) room with a bath and shower... but shower it is necessary to repair, it does not work.

Tom Where is room?

Olga On tenth floor.

Kate How much does it cost?

Olga Only 500 roubles per person, but credit cards we do not accept! Breakfast from eight o'clock to nine.

Tom Well... we want room. But is it possible to have breakfast at 7.45? By us (we have) excursion tomorrow at 8.15.

Kate And I have question. Where is it possible to drink coffee or tea? Where here café?

Olga Café from here is near, to the left, then to the right 30 metres, then straight on.

(In the café)

Ivan I am listening you (What can I get you?).

Kate For us coffee without sugar and tea with milk.

Ivan Is it all? By us (we have) sandwiches with cheese and with ham.

Tom One sandwich with cheese and one with ham, please.

Tom Cheese terrible.

Kate But ham good.

Tom Table too small.

Kate But toilets very clean.

Tom My tea cold.

Kate But waiter very beautiful (handsome).

Tom Bill, please.

Ivan Fifty roubles.

▶ F Sankt-Peeteerboorgee

In Saint Petersburg Tom and Kate are checking in at a hotel.
They speak to Olga, the receptionist at the service desk and later
to Ivan, the waiter.

Kate	Dobriiy dyen'. Oo vas yes't' nomeer na dvaeekh, na adnoo noch? Stoeet nee sleeshkam doraga?
Olga	Da, oo nas nomeer s vanay ee s dooshim... a doosh nada atreemanteeravat', on nye rabotaeet.
Tom	Gdye nomeer?
Olga	Na desyatam itazhe.
Kate	Skol'ka stoeet?
Olga	Tol'ka peet'sot rooblyeiy na cheelavyeka, no kreedeetniee kartachkee mi nye preeneemaeem! Zaftrak s vas'mee cheesof da deeveeatee.
Tom	Noo... mi khateem nomeer. A mozhna zaftrakat' f syem' sorak pyat'? Oo nas ikskoorseeya zaftra v voseem' peetnatsat.
Kate	Ee o meenya vapros. Gdye mozhna peet' kofee eelee chyaiy? Gdye z'dyes' kafe?
Olga	Kafe atsyuda bleeska, nalyeva, patom naprava treetsat myetraf, patom pryama.

(In the café)

Ivan	Slooshayu vas.
Kate	Nam kofee bees sakhara ee chyaiy s malakom.
Ivan	Eta fsyo? Oo nas bootibrodi s siram ee s veecheenoiy.
Tom	Adeen bootibrot s siram ee adeen s veecheenoiy, pazhaloosta.
Tom	Sir oozhasniiy.
Kate	A veecheena kharoshaya.
Tom	Stol sleeshkam maleenkeeiy.
Kate	A tooalyeti ocheen' cheestiee.
Tom	Moiy chyaiy khalodniy.
Kate	A afeetsiant kraseeviiy.
Tom	Shshyot, pazhaloosta.
Ivan	Peedeesyat rooblyeiy.

▶ New words

dobriiy dyen' *good day*

yes't' *there is/is there*

nomeer na dvaeekh *room for two (i.e. double room)*

na *for, on*

na adnoo noch *for one night*

nye *not*

sleeshkam *too (as in too much)*

s, z *with, from*

s vanaiy *with a bathroom*

doosh (z dooshim) *shower (with a shower)*

a *and, but*

nada *it is necessary*

atreemanteeravat' *to repair*

on *it/he*

nee rabotaeet *does not work*

na desyatam itazhe *on the tenth floor*

skol'ka *how much/how many*

tol'ka *only*

peetsot *500*

rooblee, rooblyeiy *rouble(s)*

na cheelavyeka *for a person (per person)*

kreedeetniee kartachkee *credit cards*

preeneemaeem *we accept*

zaftrak *breakfast*

s vas'mee cheesof *from eight hours (from eight o'clock)*

do, da *until*

dyeveet'/deeveetee *nine*

noo... *well...*

mi khateem *we want*

mozhna *it is possible*

zaftrakat' *to have breakfast*

syem' sorak pyat' *7.45*

ikskoorseeya *excursion*

zaftra *tomorrow*

voseem' peetnatsat *8.15*

vapros *question*

kofee *coffee*

eelee *or*

chyaiy *tea*

peet'/ya p'yu *to drink/I drink*

z'dyes' *here*

kafe *café*

atsyuda *from here*

bleeska *close, near*

nalyeva *to the left, on the left*

naprava *to the right, on the right*

treetsat myetraf *30 metres*

patom *then, next*

pryama *straight on*

slooshayu *I listen*

vi/vas *you*

nam *for us*

sakhar/sakhara *sugar*

malako/malakom *milk*

fsyo *all, everything*

bootirbrot/ bootirbrodi *sandwich/sandwiches*

sir/siram *cheese*

veecheena/veecheenoiy *ham*

oozhasniiy *terrible*

stol *table*

maleen'keeiy/maleen'kaya *small*

tooalyeti *toilets*

cheestiee *clean*

khalodniy *cold*

afeetsiant *waiter*

shshyot *bill*

peedeesyat *50*

**TOTAL NEW WORDS: 67
...only 239 words to go!**

Some useful extras

Tsifri (numerals)

adeenatsat' *11*, dveenatsat' *12*, treenatsat' *13*, cheetirnatsat' *14*,
peetnatsat' *15*, shisnatsat' *16*, seemnatsat' *17*, vaseemnatsat *18*,
deeveetnatsat' *19*, dvatsat' *20*, treetsat' *30*, sorak *40*,
peedeesyat *50*, shiz'deesyat *60*, syemdeesyat *70*, voseemdeesyat *80*,
deeveenosta *90*, sto *100*, dvyes'tee *200*, treesta *300*,
cheetireesta *400*, peetsot *500*, shisot *600*, tiseechya *1000*

You join numbers just like in English: *23* = dvatsat' tree;
35 = treetsat pyat'.

Telling the time (*vryemya*)

cheesi *clock*, tree cheesa *it is three o'clock*, f katoram cheesoo? *at
what time?*, v dva cheesa *at two o'clock*, f tree cheesa *at three
o'clock*, f pyat cheesof *at five o'clock*, (f) syem' treetsat'
(at) 7.30, meenoota *minute*, chyas *hour*, dyen' *day*, needyelya
week, myeseets *month*, got *year*

▶ Good news grammar

1 Doing things

In Week 1 you learned how to say *I, you, we... work* or *travel*.
Now let's complete the list with *he, she, it* and *they... work* or *are
working*.

Barees rabotaeet. On rabotaeet.	*Boris works. He is working.*
Ol'ga rabotaeet. Ana rabotaeet.	*Olga works. She is working.*
Teeleefon rabotaeet. On rabotaeet.	*The telephone works. It is working.*
Barees ee Ol'ga rabotayut.	*Boris and Olga work.*
Anee rabotayut.	*They are working.*

So it's '-eet' for one person and '-yut' for more than one. And if
you want to use the basic form, i.e. *to work*, it's rabotat' (with an
apostrophe at the end).

2 *To want* and *to be able to/can*

Here are two important verbs which you'll use all the time.
Unfortunately, they don't behave as well as rabotat'. I have put
them into gift boxes for you so you won't forget. Spend five
minutes on each. Use *want* instead of *would like*. It does not
sound at all rude in Russian.

khatyet' want	
ya khach**u**	*I want*
vi khat**ee**tee	*you want*
mi khat**eem**	*we want*
on, ana,	
ano khoch**eet**	*he, she, it wants*
an**ee** khat**yat**	*they want*

moch' can	
ya mag**oo**	*I can*
vi m**o**zhite	*you can*
mi m**o**zhim	*we can*
on, ana,	
ano m**o**zhit	*he, she, it can*
an**ee** mog**oo**t	*they can*

3 *Nada*: the necessary and *mozhna*: the possible

These are two very useful words. Remember when Olga said that the shower needed repairing:

    Nada atreemanteeravat'...   *It is necessary to repair...*

And then Tom wondered if they could have breakfast:

    Mozhna zaftrakat'?   *Is it possible to have breakfast?*

When you use 'nada' and 'mozhna' you'll carry on with the basic verb – just like in English. *It is necessary/possible to work/drink*: nada/mozhna rabotat'/peet', etc.

4 Word order: very relaxed!

We don't accept credit cards could be either:
    kreedeetniee kartachkee mi nee preeneemaeem.
or mi nee preeneemaeem kreedeetniye kartachkee.
Take your pick!

5 *Nyet* and *nye*

Everyone knows 'nyet' – *no?*
Its 'brother' 'nye' (*not*) is used when you are *not* doing something.

I don't work.	ya nye rabotayu.
He's not working.	on nye rabotaeet.

6 ...and now for the bad news: endings

There are three types of nouns in Russian: masculine, feminine and neuter. You can often identify which is which by the ending – usually a *consonant* (masculine), an *a* (feminine) or an o (neuter). The trouble starts when you use a noun in a sentence. Take sir: *cheese*. Take *bread with cheese*: bootirbrot s siram. Sir changes to siram. Adjectives and numbers behave equally badly: *new* could be: noviy, novim, novaya... and more! But don't despair. You'll pick them up as you go along. Mistakes are allowed and won't cramp your style.

▶ Let's speak Russian

Now let's practise what you have learned. I'll give you ten English sentences and you say them in Russian – OUT LOUD! If you have the recording, listen to check the answers. Tick each sentence if you got it right. Unless you got all ten correct, do the exercise again.

1 We would like a double room.
2 Unfortunately, it is too expensive.
3 Breakfast is at what time?
4 The telephone does not work.
5 We want sandwiches.
6 Do you also have tea?
7 Where is the café, left or right?
8 The toilets are not clean.
9 Can I please have the bill?
10 Tomorrow I go to London at nine o'clock.

Now answer in Russian. Use 'da' and 'mi' for the ones on the left and 'nyet' and 'ya' for the ones on the right.

11 Vi khateetee **ye**khat' v Maskv**oo**?
12 Oo vas z'dyes' teeleef**on**?
13 Vi khat**ee**tee yes't' (*to eat*) v v**o**seem chees**of**?

14 Vi m**o**zhitee rabotat' z**a**ftra?
15 Vi khat**ee**tee n**o**meer?

Now answer the last two using the words in brackets.

16 Gdye z'd**ye**s' kafe? (bl**ee**ska, atsy**u**da)
17 F kat**o**ram chees**oo** vi khat**ee**tee yes't'? (v shes't' s**o**rak pyat)

Answers

1 Mi khat**ee**m n**o**meer na dva**ee**kh.
2 K sazhily**e**n**ee**yu eta st**o**eet sl**ee**shkam d**o**raga.
3 Z**a**ftrak v kat**o**ram chees**oo**?
4 Tee**le**efon nye rab**o**ta**ee**t.
5 Mi khat**ee**m b**oo**tirbr**o**di.
6 A ch**yaiy** oo vas yes't'?
7 Gdye kafe, nal**ye**va **ee**lee napr**a**va?
8 Too**a**ly**e**ti nee ch**ee**sti**ee**.
9 Shsh**yo**t, pazh**a**loosta.
10 Z**a**ftra ya v L**o**ndanee v d**ye**veet chees**of**.

11 Da, mi khat**ee**m **ye**khat' v Maskv**oo**.
12 Da, oo nas z'dyes' yes't' teel**ee**fon.
13 Nyet, ya nee kh**a**chu yes't' v v**o**seem chees**of**.
14 Nyet, ya nee mag**oo** rab**o**tat' z**a**ftra.
15 Nyet, ya nee kh**a**chu n**o**meer.
16 Kafe bl**ee**ska atsy**u**da.
17 Ya kh**a**chu yes't' f shes't' s**o**rak pyat.

▶ Let's speak more Russian

Here are the two optional exercises. Remember, they may stretch the 45 minutes a day by 15 minutes. But the extra practice will be worth it.

In your own words

This exercises will teach you to express yourself freely. Use only the words you have learned so far.

Tell me in your own words that...

1 you want to know if there is availability of a double room with bath and shower
2 you want to know the price of the room for one night
3 you would like breakfast at 7.30
4 you would like to know where you can have a tea or a coffee
5 you have an excursion to Novgorod at 8.45
6 you want to know if the café is close by. Is it to the left and then straight ahead, 100 metres?
7 You want tea without sugar, a sandwich with cheese and a sandwich with ham

Tell me...

8 what you don't like about the café (awful tea, small table, dirty toilets)
9 that Kate says the waiter is good looking (Kate gavareet, shto... Kate says that...)
10 that the bill is 80 roubles

Answers

1 Oo vas yes't' nomeer na dvaeekh s vanaiy ee z dooshim?
2 Skol'ka stoeet nomeer na adnoo noch?
3 Mozhna zafrakat' v syem' treetsat'?
4 Gdye mozhna peet' chyaiy eelee kofee?
5 Oo nas ikskoorseeya v Novgarat v voseem' sorak pyat.
6 Kafe atsyuda bleeska? Kafe nalyeva, patom naprava ee pryama sto myetraf?
7 Nam chyaiy bees sakhara, bootirbrot s siram ee bootirbrot s veecheenoiy, pazhaloosta.
8 Chyaiy oozhasniiy, stol sleeshkam maleen'keeiy ee tooalyeti nye ocheen' cheestiee.
9 Kate gavareet, shto afeetsiant kraseeviiy.
10 Shshyot – voseem'deesyat rooblyeiy.

▶ Let's speak Russian – fast and fluently

Translate each section and check if it is correct. Then cover up the answers and say the three or four sentences fast!

20 seconds for a silver star, 15 seconds for a gold star.

Some of the English is in Russian-speak to help you.

Good evening. Do you have a room with bath?
700 roubles per person – too expensive.
I want room with shower.
How much costs breakfast?

Dobriiy vyecheer. Oo vas yes't' nomeer s vanaiy?
Seemsot rooblyeiy na cheelavyeka – sleeshkam doraga.
Ya khachu nomeer z dooshim.
Skol'ka stoeet zaftrak?

Bank from here very near, straight ahead, then right 20 metres.
Tomorrow at five o'clock we are going to Yalta. Do you also want to go to Yalta?
Is it possible to have breakfast at ten o'clock?

Bank atsyuda ocheen' bleeska, pryama, patom naprava dvatsat myetraf.
Zaftra f pyat cheesof mi yedeem v Yaltoo. Vi tozhe khateetee yekhat' v Yaltoo?
Mozhna zaftrakat v dyeseet' cheesof?

The room costs very expensive. Do you have a credit card?
My breakfast – cold and coffee – awful.
The bill, please. One hundred and five roubles.

Nomeer stoeet ocheen' doraga. Oo vas yes't' kreedeetnaya kartachka?
Moiy zaftrak khalodniy ee kofee oozhasniiy.
Shshyot, pazhaloosta. Sto pyat rooblyeiy.

Now say all the sentences in Russian without stopping and starting. If you can do it in under one minute you are a fast and fluent winner!

But if you are not happy with your result – just try once more.

▶ Learn by heart

Choose one of these to fill in the gaps: maeem moozhim *husband*, mayeiy zhinoiy *wife*, maeem droogam *friend*, mayeiy padroogaiy *girlfriend*. Try to say it in 45–60 seconds.

Oo meenya mala dyeneek, no...

Oo meen**ya** m**a**la* d**ye**neek, no ya khach**u o**tpoosk v m**a**ee.

Ya khach**u ye**khat' f Sankt-Peeteerb**oo**rk s...

Ya khach**u** f Sankt-Peeteerb**oo**rgee peet' mn**o**ga** shamp**a**nskava ee yes't' b**oo**tirbr**o**di. **E**ta vazm**o**zhna***? Da, **e**ta need**o**raga st**o**eet. Tol'ka d**ye**seet' t**i**seech roobl**ye**iy na cheelav**ye**ka, ee oo meen**ya** yes't' kreed**ee**tnaya k**a**rtachka...

---

*mala: *a little* **mnoga: *a lot, many* ***vazmozhna: *it is possible*

Test your progress

Translate these sentences into Russian and write them out. See what you can remember without looking at the previous pages. (Remember. Don't highlight the part of the word which is stressed.)

1 I drink a lot of champagne.
2 How much is (costs) breakfast, please?
3 Is there a travel agency here?
4 Do you have a table? At 7.15?
5 I would like to drink (some) coffee.
6 My holiday in Florida was better.
7 Where is there a good hotel?
8 Can I have the telephone bill, please?
9 We were in Saint Petersburg in May.
10 My house is too big.
11 At what time are you in Moscow tomorrow?
12 I am there from eight until five.
13 Excuse me, please. Where are the toilets, straight ahead?
14 We want to travel to Oslo in January, but it is too cold.
15 Does that cost more money?
16 Tomorrow where are you at 10.30?
17 It's terrible. The (hotel) room is very expensive.
18 Is it possible to drink coffee here now? Do you have seats?
19 We have a small house in America, but it is very expensive.
20 Goodbye, we are going to Yalta.

Check your answers with the Key on page 87 and work out your score. Now enter your result on the Progress chart in the front of the book. If it is above 70% you have done very well.

03

week three

Study for 45 minutes a day – but there are no penalties for doing more!

Day one

- Read **Let's go shopping**.
- Listen to/Read **Mi dyelaeem pakoopkee**.
- Listen to/Read the **New words**, then learn some of them.

Day two

- Repeat **Mi dyelaeem pakoopkee** and the **New words**.
- Learn all the **New words**. Use the **Flash cards**!

Day three

- Test yourself on all the **New words** – boring, boring, but you are over halfway already!
- Read and learn the **Good news grammar**.
- Go over the **Good news grammar**.

Day four

- Listen to/Read **Learn by heart**.
- Cut out and learn the ten **Flash sentences**.

Day five

- Listen to/Read **Spot the keys**.
- Listen to/Read **Let's speak Russian**.

Day six

- Go over **Learn by heart**.
- Have a quick look at **New words**, weeks 1–3. You now know over 200 words! Well, more or less.
- Listen to/Read **Let's speak more Russian** (optional).
- Listen to/Read **Let's speak Russian – fast and fluently** (optional).
- Translate **Test your progress**.

Day seven – enjoy your day off!

day-by-day guide

Let's go shopping

Tom and Kate are staying in Moscow. Kate is planning some shopping. (The English is in 'Russian-speak' to get you tuned in.)

Kate Well, today for us it is necessary to do shopping. First we go to centre of town on bus.

Tom But weather bad. (It is) Cold. And on television much sport. At 12.30 goes (is on) golf...

Kate Sorry, but for us it is necessary (to go) to bank, to post office for stamps, to chemist's, to dry cleaner's and to supermarket.

Tom Well, golf not possible to watch... perhaps football at three o'clock. Is that all?

Kate No, for us it is necessary also (to go) to department store for new suitcase and to hairdresser's. And I want also (to go) to jewellery shop and to shop of souvenirs.

Tom Good grief! Shops open until what time?

Kate Until six or until eight, it seems.

Tom Ah, football also not possible to watch... perhaps tennis at 8.30...

(Later)

Kate It seems, I too many presents bought. Bottle of champagne, tin of caviar, Russian dolls, chocolate.

Tom No problem! For us it is necessary to buy many presents. But what there, in big bag? Is it for me?

Kate And yes and no. I was in jewellery shop, then in department store. In jewellery shop I saw brooch. It is amber brooch. Splendid, isn't it true? Shop assistant was very pleasant and so handsome as Tom Cruise.

Tom Who such (who is) Tom Cruise? And how much costs brooch?

Kate A little expensive... 600 roubles.

Tom What?... Crazy!

Kate But here is T-shirt. It costs not very expensive. And here's English newspaper... and on television now is going (is on) tennis, isn't it true?

▶ Mi dyelaeem pakoopkee

Tom and Kate are staying in Moscow. Kate is planning some shopping.

Kate Noo, seevodnya nam nada dyelat' pakoopkee. Snachyala mi **ye**deem f tsentr gorada na avtoboosee.

Tom No pagoda plakhaya. Kholadna. Ee po teeleeveezaroo mnoga sporta. V dveenatsat treetsat eedyot gol'f...

Kate Ezveenee, no nam nada v bank, na pochtoo za markamee, v aptyekoo, f kheemcheestkoo ee f soopeermarkeet.

Tom Noo, gol'f neel'zya smatryet'... mozhit bit' footbol f tree cheesa. Eta fsyo?

Kate Nyet, nam nada tozhe v ooneeveermak za novim cheemadanam ee f pareekmakheerskooyu. Ee ya khachu v yuveeleerniy magazeen ee v magazeen sooveeneeraf.

Tom Bozhe moiy! Magazeeni atkriti da kakova chyasa?

Kate Da shes't'**ee ee**lee da vas'mee, kazhitsa.

Tom Akh, foodbol tozhe neel'zya smatryet'... mozhit bit' tenees v voseem' treetsat'...

(Later)

Kate Kazhetsa, ya sleeshkam mnoga padarkaf koopeela. Bootilkoo shampanskava, bankoo eekri, matryoshkee, shikalat.

Tom Nyet prablyem! Nam nada koopeet' mnoga padarkaf. A shto tam v balshoiy soomkee? Eta dlya meenya?

Kate Ee da ee nyet. Ya bila v yuveeleernam magazeenee, patom v ooneeveermagee. V yuveeleernam magazeenee ya ooveedeela broshkoo. Eta yantarnaya broshka. Preekrasnaya, nye pravda lee? Pradavyets bil ocheen' preeyatniiy ee takoiy zhe krasaveets, kak Tom Cruise.

Tom Kto takoiy Tom Cruise? Ee skol'ka stoeet broshka?

Kate Neemnoshka doraga. Shisot (600) rooblyeiy.

Tom Shto? S ooma sashla!

Kate No vot foodbolka. Stoeet nye ocheen' doraga. A vot angleeskaya gazyeta... a po teeleeveezaroo seechyas eedyot tenees, nye pravda lee?

▶ New words

Learn the **New words** in half the time using flash cards. There are 22 to start you off. Get a friend to make the rest!

seev**o**dnya *today*
d**ye**lat' *to do*
pak**oo**pkee *the shopping*
snach**ya**la *first*
ts**e**ntr *centre*
aft**o**boos/aft**o**boosee *bus*
pag**o**da *weather*
plakh**a**ya *bad*
kh**o**ladna *cold*
po, pa *on, along, according to*
teeleev**ee**zar/teeleev**ee**zaroo *television*
sp**o**rt/sp**o**rta/sp**o**rtoo *sport*
eed**yo**t *(he, she) it goes, is going*
eezveen**ee** *I am sorry (informal)*
p**o**chta/p**o**chtoo *post office*
za *for, behind, beyond*
m**a**rkee/m**a**rkamee *stamps*
apt**ye**ka/apt**ye**koo *chemist's*
kheemch**ee**stka/kheemch**ee**stkoo *dry cleaner's*
soop**ee**rmarkeet *supermarket*
neel'**zya** *it is not possible, one may not*
smatr**ye**t' *to watch*
m**o**zhit bit' *perhaps*
f tree ch**ee**sa *at three o'clock*
ooneev**ee**rmag/ooneev**ee**rmagee *department store*
n**o**viy/n**o**vim *new*
cheemad**a**n/cheemad**a**nam *suitcase*
pareekmakh**ee**rskaya/ pareekmakh**ee**rskooyu *hairdresser's*
yuvel**ee**rniy *jewellery (adj)*
magaz**ee**n/magaz**ee**nee *shop/shops*
soov**ee**n**ee**ri/soov**ee**n**ee**raf *souvenirs*

B**o**zhe moiy! *Good grief!* (lit: *God my!*)
atkr**i**ti *open (plural form)*
da kak**o**va ch**ya**sa? *until when?*
k**a**zhitsa *it seems, I think/believe*
ten**ee**s *tennis*
mn**o**ga *many*
koop**ee**la *(I) bought*
boot**i**lkoo shamp**a**nskava *bottle (of) champagne*
shamp**a**nskaye *champagne*
pad**a**rkee/pad**a**rkaf *presents*
b**a**nka/b**a**nkoo *tin, jar*
eekra/**ee**kri *caviar*
matr**yo**shka/matr**yo**shkee *Russian doll/dolls (fit one inside other)*
shikal**a**t *chocolate*
nyet prabl**ye**m! *no problem!*
koop**ee**t'/koop**ee**la *to buy/she bought*
shto *what, that*
s**oo**mka, s**oo**mkee/pak**ye**teek *bag*
dlya meen**ya** *for me*
oov**ee**deet'/oov**ee**deela *to see/she saw*
br**o**shka/br**o**shkoo *brooch*
yant**a**rnaya *amber*
preekr**a**snaya *splendid*
nye pr**a**vda lee *isn't it?*
pradav**ye**ts *shop assistant*
pree**ya**tniiy *pleasant*
tak**oi**y zhe … kak *just as … as*
kras**a**veets *handsome fellow*
kto tak**oi**y… ? *Who is… ?*
neemn**o**shka *a little*
s **oo**ma sashl**a** *crazy! (to a man one would say: s **oo**ma sash**o**l)*

vot   *here (there) is/are*
foodbolka   *T-shirt*

angleeskaya/Angleeya,
   Anglee-ee   *English/England*
gazyeta   *newspaper*

**TOTAL NEW WORDS: 67
...only 172 words to go!**

More extras

Tsveeta (colours)

byeliiy	*white*	zeelyoniiy	*green*
chyorniiy .	*black*	aranzhiviiy	*orange*
krasniiy	*red*	rozaviiy	*pink*
seeneey	*blue*	syeriiy	*grey*
zholtiiy	*yellow*	kareechneeviiy	*brown*

▶ Spot the keys

By now you can say many things in Russian. But what happens if you ask a question and don't understand the answer – hitting you at the speed of an automatic rifle? The smart way is not to panic, but to listen out for the words you know. Any familiar words which you pick up will provide you with key words – clues to what the other person is saying.

If you have the recording listen to the dialogue. If you don't – read on. You are trying to ask the way to the post office...

You   Eezveeneetee, pazhaloosta, gdye pochta?
Answer *Noo, eta nye tak prosta.* *Snachyala eedeetee* pryama da *slyedooshcheevapeereekryostka, tamgdyenakhodeetsa* balshoiy krasniiy dom. Patom nalyeva, *vi ooveedeetee tam eeshshyo* magazeeni. *Eeshshyopadalshye eedeetye naprava.* *Vi ooveedeetee* aptyekoo *naproteef* pochti.

Did you hear the key words? pryama da – balshoiy krasniiy dom – patom – nalyeva – magazeeni – aptyekoo – pochti.

I think you'll get there!

▶ Good news grammar

1 The past

This is easier than in French! Here's a very basic 'recipe':

- Take the basic form of the verb, say, rabotat'.
- Take off the 't' and add an 'l' if you are talking about one male person (it could be Boris or yourself): Barees rabotal.
- Add 'la' for one female person (it could be Tanya or you): Tanya rabotala.
- Add 'lo' for neuter nouns: radeea ne rabotalo (pronounced rabotala).
- Add 'lee' for you (vi) and everything that's more than one: Boris and Tanya, we, they... rabotalee.

Most important: learn all the sample phrases which are in the past.

2 *Nada, mozhna* and *neel'zya*

Remember 'nada' and 'mozhna' from Week 2? *It is necessary. It is possible.* Here's another one: 'neel'zya': *it's forbidden,* so *it's not possible.*

These three are very useful when you want to say *can, can't* or *must,* because that's really what they express: *I can... for me it's possible. I can't... for me it's not possible. I must... for me it's necessary.*

So all you need to do now is to add: *for me, for you, for us* etc. Here's the full list using *nada* and *must buy* as an example:

mnye nada koopeet'	*for me it is necessary... I must buy*
vam nada koopeet'	*for you it is necessary... you must buy*
nam nada koopeet'	*for us it is necessary... we must buy*
yemoo/yeiy nada koopeet'	*for him/her it is necessary... he/she must buy*
eem nada koopeet'	*for them it is necessary... they must buy.*

So now you can mix and match. Mnye mozhna koopeet': *I can buy.* Nam neel'zya rabotat': *We can't work.*

3 To go: *eetee'* on foot and *yekhat'* by transport

Here's another gift box to help you remember these two:

eetee'		yekhat'
ya eed**oo**	*I go*	ya **ye**doo
vi eed**yo**tee	*you go*	vi **ye**deetee
on, ana eed**yo**t	*he, she goes*	on, ana **ye**deet
mi eed**yom**	*we go*	mi **ye**deem
an**ee** eed**oot**	*they go*	an**ee** **ye**doot

▶ Learn by heart

Say these seven lines in under 50 seconds. The more expression you use the easier it will be to remember all the useful bits.

Seev**o**dnya nam n**a**da d**ye**lat' pak**oo**pkee – nyet prabl**ye**m!
No atk**oo**da* **ye**deet aft**o**boos v magaz**ee**ni?
Akh, b**o**zhe moiy! K**a**zhitsa, oo m**ee**n**ya** m**a**la d**ye**neek.
Mi koop**ee**lee mn**o**ga pad**a**rkaf: mat**ryo**shkee, br**o**shkoo ee b**a**nkoo **ee**kri.
Eta b**i**la d**o**roga: sh**e**ssot roobl**ye**iy, no pradav**ye**ts bil **o**cheen' pree**ya**tniy.

*atkooda: *from where*

▶ Let's speak Russian

Over to you! If you have the recording, listen to check your answers. Always answer OUT LOUD! Start with a ten-point warm-up. Say in Russian:

1 Now I am going to (the) post office.
2 Until what time (are the) shops open?
3 I am sorry, but that is too expensive.
4 From where bus goes to centre?
5 We bought souvenirs in Novgorod.
6 Can one buy caviar in the supermarket?
7 Shopping without money? No, but I have (a) credit card.
8 I everything bought in the department store.
9 We must watch the weather on television.
10 Good grief! The television doesn't work!

Answer the following using the words in brackets.

11 Oo vas yes't' seenee-ee foodbolkee? (da, oo nas)
12 Vi koopeelee markee f soopeermarkeetee? (da, mi)
13 Vi rabotalee v bankee? (nyet, mi)
14 Vam nada eetee v dyeveet cheesof? (nyet, nam)
15 Oo vas mnoga dyeneek? (nyet, oo nas, mala)
16 Shto vi koopeelee? Shikalat eelee shampanskaye? (shikalat)
17 Kto smatryel foodbol po teeleeveezaroo? (ya)
18 Da kakova chyasa magazeenee atkriti? (vas'mee cheesof)

Answers

1 Seechyas ya eedoo na pochtoo.
2 Magazeeni atkriti da kakova chyasa?
3 Ezveeneetee no eta sleeshkam doraga.
4 Atkooda aftoboos yedeet f tsentr?
5 Mi koopeelee sooveeneeri v Novgaradee.
6 Mozhna koopeet' eekroo f soopeermarkeetee?
7 Dyelat' pakoopkee bees dyeneek? Nyet, no oo meenya yes't' kreedeetnaya kartachka.
8 Ya fsyo koopeela f ooneeveermagee.
9 Nam nada smatryet' pagodoo po teeleeveezaroo.
10 Bozhe moiy! Teeleeveezar nee rabotaeet!
11 Da, oo nas yes't' seenee-ee foodbolkee.
12 Da, mi koopeelee markee f soopeermarkeetee.
13 Nyet, mi nee rabotalee v bankee.
14 Nyet, nam nee nada eetee f dyeveet cheesof.
15 Nyet, oo nas mala dyeneek.
16 Mi koopeelee (ya koopeel/ya koopeela) shikalat.
17 Ya smatryel/ya smatryela foodbol po teeleeveezaroo.
18 Da vas'mee (cheesof).

▶ Let's speak more Russian

Here are the two optional exercises. Remember, they may stretch the 45 minutes a day by 15 minutes. But the extra practice will be worth it.

In your own words

This exercise will teach you to express yourself freely. Use only the words you have learned so far.

Tell me in your own words that...

1 today you must go shopping
2 first you are going to the centre of town by bus
3 unfortunately you have little money, but you do have a credit card
4 you have to go to the supermarket to buy a bottle of champagne
5 then you have to go to the department store to buy Russian dolls
6 you bought caviar, coffee and chocolate in the supermarket
7 it was very expensive; it seems now you have little money
8 you watched the weather on television
9 the sandwiches cost fifteen roubles; that was not expensive
10 you have bought too many presents

Answers

1 Seevodnya mnye nada dyelat' pakoopkee.
2 Snachyala ya yedoo f tsentr gorada na aftoboosee.
3 K sazhilyeneeu oo meenya mala dyeneek, no oo meenya kreedeetnaya kartachka.
4 Mnye nada v soopeermarkeet koopeet' bootilkoo shampanskava.
5 Patom mnye nada v ooneeveermak koopeet' matryoshkee.
6 Ya koopeel/koopeela eekroo, kofee ee shikalat f soopeermarkeetee.
7 Eta bila ocheen' doraga. Kazhitsa, seechyas oo meenya mala dyeneek.
8 Ya smatryel/smatryela pagodoo po teeleeveezaroo.
9 Bootirbrodi stoeelee peetnatsat rooblyeiy. Eta bila nyedoraga.
10 Ya sleeshkam mnoga podarkaf koopeel/koopeela.

▶ Let's speak Russian – fast and fluently

Translate each section and check if it is correct. Then cover up the answers and say the three or four sentences fast! Some of the English is in 'Russian-speak' to help you.

20 seconds per section for a silver star, 15 seconds for a gold star.

Good grief! Is that an English newspaper?
Do you want to watch football or tennis?
Did you watch the sport on the television?

Bozhe moiy! Eta angleeskaya gazyeta?
Vi khateetee smatryet' foodbol eelee tenees?
Vi smatryeli sport po teeleeveezaroo?

From where bus goes to university?
Excuse me, are you going to the pharmacy?
Where can I buy stamps?
We must buy souvenirs in department store.

Atkooda aftoboos eedyot v ooneeveerseetyet?
Eezveeneetee, vi eedyotee v aptyekoo?
Gdye mozhna koopeet' markee?
Nam nada koopit' sooveeneeri v ooneeveermagee.

Today the weather is good.
I don't need to go at six o'clock.
Today you mustn't work. You must go shopping.

Seevodnya pagoda kharoshaya.
Mnye nee nada eetee f shes't' cheesof.
Seevodnya vam neel'zya rabotat'. Vam nada dyelat' pakoopkee.

Now say all the sentences in Russian without stopping and starting. If you can do it all in under one minute you are a fast and fluent winner!

But if you are not happy with your result – just try once more.

Test your progress

Translate these sentences into Russian. Then check your answers and be amazed!

1 Where is (the) sales assistant?
2 Where is it possible to buy sandwiches?
3 When must you (go) to England today? At seven o'clock?
4 We saw that yesterday on television.
5 Now (the) shops (are) open, it seems.
6 Here there is (a) department store or supermarket?
7 Excuse me, are you also going to the post office?
8 Where did you buy (the) English newspaper?
9 Do you want coffee or tea?
10 The weather is bad today. It is not possible to go to Novgorod.
11 That is all? That was not expensive.
12 The stamps cost 15 roubles.
13 We accept credit cards.
14 Is 300 grams (of) cheese too much? No, no problem.
15 There is (a) new dry cleaner's near here.
16 Do you have (a) bag for my T-shirt, please?
17 I saw here (a) chemist's, it seems.
18 Good grief! (The) bus has broken down (isn't working) and (the) Mercedes also has broken down (isn't working)!
19 Did you see (the) T-shirt? Where did you buy it?
20 Five hundred roubles, but I have only dollars.

04

week four

Study for 45 minutes a day but if you are keen try 50... 55...!

Day one

- Read **We are going to the restaurant**.
- Listen to/Read **Mi eedyom v reestaran**.
- Read the **New words**. Learn the easy ones.

Day two

- Repeat the dialogue. Learn the harder **New words**.
- Cut out the **Flash words** to help you.

Day three

- Learn all the **New words** until you know them well.
- Read and learn the **Good news grammar**.

Day four

- Listen to/Read **Learn by heart**.
- Cut out and learn the ten **Flash sentences**.

Day five

- Listen to/Read **Spot the keys**.
- Read **Say it simply**.

Day six

- Listen to/Read **Let's speak Russian**.
- Listen to/Read **Let's speak more Russian** (optional).
- Listen to/Read **Let's speak Russian – fast and fluently** (optional).
- Translate **Test your progress**.

Day seven

Are you keeping your scores above 60%? In that case... **have a good day off!**

day-by-day guide

We are going to (the) restaurant

Tom and Kate are still in Moscow. Boris Vadimovich is inviting them to dinner. (The English is in 'Russian-speak' to get you tuned in.)

Kate Tom, someone rang. He did not say why. Number is on paper, by telephone. Some Boris…

Tom Oh, yes, Boris Vadimovich, good customer of our firm. I him well know. Very pleasant person. By me meeting with him on Thursday. Very important matter.

Tom *(On the phone)* Hello, good morning, Boris Vadimovich… Speaks Tom Walker… Yes, thank you… yes, of course, it is possible… next week… of course… yes… very interesting… no, by us time there is… splendid… no, only for a few days… I understand… when?… at 8 o'clock… upstairs by exit, by door. Well, until Tuesday, thank you very much, goodbye.

Kate What are we doing on Tuesday?

Tom We are going to restaurant with Boris Vadimovich. Restaurant in centre behind church. He says, that restaurant new. Boris Vadimovich in Moscow for two days, with Edith and Peter Palmer from our firm.

Kate I know Edith Palmer. She is boring and knows everything. She has a terrible dog. I think, that on Tuesday I will be ill. Heavy cold and everything hurts. The doctor necessary it will be to call…

Tom Please, (one can't do that) thus it is not possible; it's not on. Boris Vadimovich is very important client.

(In the restaurant)

Waiter Here's the menu. Today by us also firm's dishes (specials) – fish, and for sweet course – walnut cake.

Boris What for you, Mrs Walker? Soup you want? Meat or fish?

Kate For me steak with salad, please.

Edith To eat much red meat is harmful, Kate.

Boris Mr Walker, what for you? And what you want to drink? Wine?

Tom Beer, then sausage with fried potato, please.

┈┈➡ Page 52

▶ Mi eedyom v reestaran

Tom and Kate are still in Moscow. Boris Vadeemaveech is inviting them to dinner.

Kate	Tom, kto-ta pazvaneel. On nee skazal, pacheemoo. Nomeer na boomagee, okala teeleefona. Kakoiy-ta Barees.
Tom	Akh, da, Barees Vadeemaveech, kharoshiiy kleeyent nashiiy feermi. Ya yeevo kharasho znayu. Ocheen' preeyatniy cheelavyek. Oo meenya fstryechya s neem f cheetvyerk. Ocheen' vazhniee deela.
Tom	*(On the phone)* Alo, dobraye ootra, Barees Vadeemaveech. Gavareet Tom Walker... Da, spaseeba... da, kanyeshna vazmozhna... na slyedooshshyeeiy needyele... kanyeshna... da... ocheen' eenteeryesna... nyet, oo nas vryemya yes't'... preekrasna... nyet, tol'ka na nyeskal'ka dnyeiy... Ya paneemayu... kagda?... v voseem' cheesof... naveerkhoo, okala vikhada, okala dveeree. Noo, do ftorneeka, spaseeba balshoye, da sveedaneeya.
Kate	Shto mi dyelaeem va ftorneek?
Tom	Mi eedyom v reestaran s Bareesam Vadeemaveecheem. Reestaran f tsentree, za tserkav'yu. On gavareet, shto reestaran noviy. Barees Vadeemaveech v Maskvye na dva dnya, s Edith i Peeterom Palmer eez nashiiy feermi.
Kate	Ya znayu Edith Palmer. Ana skoochnaya ee fsyo znayet loochshye vsyekh. Oo neeyo oozhasnaya sabaka. Ya doomayu, shto va ftorneek ya boodoo bal'na. Prastooda ee fsyo baleet. Vrachya nada boodeet vizvat'...
Tom	Pazhalusta, tak neel'zya, tak nye gadeetsa. Barees Vadeemaveech ocheen' vazhniiy kleeyent.

(In the restaurant)

Waiter	Vot meenyu. Seevodnya oo nas tozhe feermeeniee blyuda – riba, ee na slatkaye – aryekhaviy tort.
Boris	Shto vam, gaspazha Walker? Soop khateetee? Myasa eelee riboo?
Kate	Mnye beefshteks s salatam, pazhaloosta.
Edith	Yes't' mnoga tyomnava myasa vryedna, Kate.
Boris	Gaspadeen Walker, shto vam? Ee shto vi khateetye peet'? Veeno?
Tom	Peeva, patom kalbasoo z zhareenaiy kartoshkaiy, pazhaloosta.

······➡ Page 53

Edith	But Tom, that's very greasy! I would not want to eat such dishes.
Boris	And you, Mrs Palmer?
Edith	Small piece of chicken from grill, fruit and glass of water.
(Later…)	
Boris	Everyone ready? It is already late. Who wants coffee? No one? Good, bill, please.
Edith	Oh, Boris Vadimovich, you can me help, please? How in Russian 'doggy bag'? I want bag for my dog.
Kate	But Edith, your dog in England!

▶ New words

kto-ta *someone*
pazvan**ee**t'/pazvan**eel** *to ring/he rang*
on/y**e**vo/n**eem** *he, him*
skaz**at**'/skaz**al** *to say/he said*
pachem**oo** *why*
n**o**meer *number*
b**oo**maga/boom**agee** *paper*
okala *near, by*
kak**oiy**-ta *some (sort of)*
kle**ey**ent *customer*
kharash**o** *good, well*
f**eerma**/f**eermi** *firm*
znat'/zn**ayu**/zn**aeet** *to know/ I know/he/(she) knows*
cheelav**yek** *person*
fstry**e**chya *meeting*
cheetv**yerk** *Thursday*
v**azh**niee *important*
d**ye**la *matter*
gavar**ee**t'/gavar**ee**t *to speak, to say/he speaks, he says*
spas**eeba**/balsh**oiy**e *thank you/very much*
kan**ye**shna *of course*
vazm**o**zhna *it is possible*
sl**ye**dooshshy**ee**iy *next*
eent**ee**ry**esna** *it is interesting*
vr**ye**mya *time*

ny**e**skal'ka *a few*
dny**eiy**/d**n**ya *days*
kagd**a** *when*
nave**e**rkh**oo** *upstairs*
v**i**khad/v**i**khada *exit*
dv**yer**/dv**ee**ree *door*
ft**o**rneek/ft**o**rneeka *Tuesday*
ts**e**rkaf'/ts**e**rkav'yu *church*
oozh**a**snaya *terrible*
sab**a**ka *dog*
d**oo**mat'/d**oo**mayu *to think/ I think*
b**oo**doo/b**oo**deet *I will be/he (she, it) will be*
bal'n**a** *ill, sick*
prast**oo**da *a cold*
bal**ee**t *it hurts*
vrach/vr**a**chya *doctor*
v**i**zvat'… *to summon, call, send for*
tak *thus, so*
nee gad**ee**tsa *it does not fit (it's not on)*
meen**yu** *menu*
f**ee**rm**ee**niee bly**u**da *firm's dishes (i.e. specials)*
r**i**ba/r**i**boo *fish*
sl**a**tkaye *sweet, dessert*
ary**e**khaviy tort *walnut cake*
gasp**a**zha *Mrs*

Edith	No Tom, eta ocheen' zhirna! Ya nye khatyela bi yes't' takoye blyuda.
Boris	A vi, gaspazha Palmer?
Edith	Maleenkiy koosochyek kooreetsi, z greelya, frookti ee stakan vadi.
(Later...)	
Boris	Fsye gatovi? Oozhe pozna. Kto khocheet kofee? Neekto? Kharasho, shshyot, pazhaloosta.
Edith	Akh, Barees Vadeemaveech, vi nee mozhitee mnye pamoch, pazhaloosta? Kak pa-rooskee 'doggy bag'? Ya khachu pakyeteek dlya mayeiy sabakee.
Kate	No Edith, vasha sabaka v Anglee-ee!

soop	*soup*	koosocheek	*piece*
myasa	*meat*	kooreetsa/kooreetsi	*chicken*
beefshteks	*steak*	greel'/greelya	*grill*
salat/salatam	*salad*	frookt	*fruit*
tyomnava myasa	*dark (red) meat*	stakan	*glass*
vryedna	*it is harmful*	vada/vadi	*water*
gaspadeen	*Mr*	gatovi	*ready*
veeno	*wine*	oozhe	*already*
peeva	*beer*	pozna	*it is late*
kalbasa/kalbasoo	*sausage*	neekto	*no one*
zhareenaiy kartoshkaiy	*fried*	pamoch'	*to help*
potato		kak pa-rooskee	*how in*
zhirna	*it is greasy*		*Russian*

TOTAL NEW WORDS: 74
...only 98 words to go!

▶ Last extras

Days of the week

paneedyel'neek	*Monday*	pyatneetsa	*Friday*
ftorneek	*Tuesday*	soobota	*Saturday*
sreeda	*Wednesday*	vaskreesyen'ye	*Sunday*
cheetvyerk	*Thursday*		

To say: *on* Monday/Tuesday/Wednesday... etc. you add 'f' (or 'va' for Tuesday): f paneedyel'neek, va ftorneek, f sryedoo, f cheetvyerk, f pyatneetsoo, f soobotoo, v vaskreesyen'ye. Some of the endings change... Spot the differences!

▶ Good news grammar

1 Pronouns – useful!

These are worth learning because you'll need them all the time.

I = ya	*me* = meen**ya**	*to/for me* = mnye	*with me* = sa mnoiy
you = vi	*you* = vas	*to/for you* = vam	*with you* = s v**a**mee
he = on	*him* = yeev**o**	*to/for him* = yem**oo**	*with him* = s neem
she = an**a**	*her* = yee**yo**	*to/for her* = yeiy	*with her* = s nyeiy
we = mi	*us* = nas	*to/for us* = nam	*with us* = s n**a**mee
they = an**ee**	*them* = eekh	*to for them* = eem	*with them* = s n**ee**mee

Learn one row at a time – down or across. Then put each word on a flash card and invest ten minutes a day. By the end of the week you'll know the lot!

2 The future – easy!

If you want to talk about something that is going to happen in the future, you could get away with using the present tense.

Mi yedeem f tsentr. *We are going to the centre/*
We'll go to the centre.

Seevodnya ya eedoo *Today I am going (will go)*
 f reestaran. *to the restaurant.*

But if you want to say: *I'll, you'll,* or *he'll be...,* you say: ya boodoo, on boodeet, vi boodeetye:

Va ftorneek ya boodoo bal'na. *On Tuesday I will be ill.*

3 I would – would you?

To say *would* in Russian is fairly simple. Let's say: *I would buy...*
You take the past tense of *buy: bought* = koopeela – and add the word **bi:**

Ya koopeela bi... *I would buy...*
Ana khatyela bi... *She would like...*
Barees skazal bi... *Boris would say...*

Easy!

4 Short cut! Leaving out the verb 'to go'

There's another bonus when using nada, mozhna or neelz'ya.

When you say that *it's necessary, possible* or *not possible to go somewhere* you can leave out the go: Nam nada v bank. *It's necessary for us (to go) to the bank.* Good shortcut!

5 Being polite

If you ask a question and want to be polite you use the negative.

So, instead of asking: *Could you help me?*, you'll say Y*ou could not help me, (by any chance, could you)?* i.e. Vi nee mozhitee mnye pamoch'?.

Vi nee znaeetee, gdye komnata 3? *You don't know where room 3 is (by any chance, do you)?*

6 *na, do, po, s, v, za*: Lots for the price of a few!

These little words which tell you where things are (also known as prepositions) are most generous: each one has several meanings! Take 'na'. It can mean: *on, onto, to, at* and *for*. Here are some others:

do, da	*until, before, as far as*	s, z	*with, from*
po, pa	*along, on, according to*	v, f, va	*in, into, to, at*
za	*for, beyond, behind*		

Unfortunately, these prepositions do terrible things to the ending of the next word. But don't worry, you'll remember those when you learn your **Flash sentences** and **Learn by heart**.

▶ Learn by heart

This is a telephone call by a rather opinionated person... When you have learned it by heart try to act it out in less than a minute.

> **Vi khateetee eetee sa mnoiy v reestaran?**
> Ya znayu adeen ocheen' kharoshiiy reestaran.
> Tam mozhna ocheen' vkoosna* payes't' ee veeno preekrasnaye.
> Nyet, vi nee khateetye? Pacheemoo nyet? Ya ocheen' eenteeryesniiy cheelavyek!
> Vi meenya nee znaeetee?
> No kanyeshna, vi veedeetee** meenya po teeleeveezaroo.
> Vi ne mozhitee? Pacheemoo nyet?
> Oo vas vazhnaye fstryechya?
> Eta neevazmozhna!

*fkoosna: *delicious* (the most commonly used word in Russian when praising food)

** veedeet'/veedeetee: *to see/you see*

▶ Spot the keys

This time you are in a department store and ask the sales assistant if the red T-shirt you fancy is also available in a size 40 (sarakavova razmyera).

You   Eezveeneeti, pazhaloosta, oo vas yes't' eta foodbolka sarakavova razmyera?

She says 'nyet', then 'meenootachkoo, pazhaloosta' and goes into the stockroom. When she comes back, this is what she says:

Answer   *Noo, oonas takikh* foodbolok *astayotsaocheen'mala, oo nas seeychas* tol'ka zholtiee sarakavova razmyera. *Noo oonasyes't'yeeshshyo* krasniye foodbolkee treetsat' vas'mova razmyera. *Ee stil'takoiy,shtoyabiskazala,shto* treetsat' vas'moiy razmyer vam gadeetsa.

Did you get the key words? Size 40 was only available in yellow. They have red in 38, which should fit.

Say it simply

When people want to speak Russian but don't dare, it's usually because they are trying to *translate* what they want to say from English into Russian. And when they don't know some of the words, they give up!

With **Instant Russian** you work around the words you don't know with the words you do know!

Believe me, with some 400 words you can say anything!

It may not always be very elegant, but you are communicating!

Here are two examples showing you how to say things in a simple way. Words that are not part of the **Instant** vocabulary are in **bold**.

1 You need to **change** your **flight** from Tuesday to Friday.

   Mi nye mozhim **ye**khat' va f**t**orneek. Mi khateem samalyot f pyatneetsoo.

or

   Ftorneek nam nee gadeetsa. Mi khateem **ye**khat' f pyatneetsoo.

2 Your **watch** is **broken** and you need to have it mended before you leave.

   Eezveeneetee, pazhaloosta, nada atreemanteeravat' cheesi, anee nee rabotayut. Z'dyes' yes't' magazeen, gdye mozhna skaryeye atreemanteeravat' eekh?

▶ Let's speak Russian

Here are ten sentences to warm-up, and then on to greater things!

1 Who has said that?
2 I don't know why.
3 You to help? (can I help you?)
4 We have time – on Monday, I believe.
5 I want to drive to Moscow.
6 He would like to know that.
7 Work on Sunday? That's not on!
8 Do you want my number?
9 Chicken for me, please.
10 Yes, of course, I have an appointment.

Now pretend you are in Russia with friends who do not speak Russian. They will want you to ask people things in Russian, such as 'Please ask him...'

11 if he knows Edith Palmer.
12 if he is going to the restaurant with us on Tuesday.
13 if she would like meat or fish and fried potato.
14 if they have an appointment today.
15 if they know where the restaurant is.

Now they ask you to tell people things. This time there may be words you don't know, so you have to use your **Instant** words. They say: 'Please tell her...'

16 that the soup is very delicious.
17 that unfortunately the shower is not in working order.
18 that we would like a meal with them.
19 that you are allergic to fish.
20 that Saturday will suit us.

Answers

1 Kto skazal eta?
2 Ya ne znayu, pacheemoo.
3 Vam pamoch'?
4 Oo nas vryemya yes't' – f paneedyel'neek, kazhitsa.
5 Ya khachu yekhat' v Maskvoo.
6 On khatyel bi znat' eta.
7 Rabotat' v vaskreesyen'ye? Tak nye gadeetsa.
8 Vi khateetee moiy nomeer?
9 Mnye kooreetsoo, pazhaloosta.
10 Da, kanyeshna, oo meenya fstryechya.

11 Vi znaeetee Edith Palmer?
12 Vi eedyotee s namee v reestaran va ftorneek?
13 Vi khateetee myasa eelee riboo z zhareenaiy kartoshkaiy?
14 Yes't' oo vas fstryechya seevodnya.
15 Vi nee znaeetee, gdye reestaran?
16 Soop ocheen' fkoosniy.
17 K sazhilyeneeyu doosh nye rabotaeet.
18 Mozhna eetee v reestaran?
19 On/ana nee yes't' riboo.
20 Soobota nam gadeetsa.

▶ Let's speak more Russian

For these optional exercises add an extra 15 minutes to your daily schedule. And remember: near enough is good enough!

In your own words

This exercise will teach you to express yourself freely. Use only the words you have learned so far.

Tell me in your own words that...

1 Mr Ivanov rang you
2 he is a good client of your firm
3 you are going to a restaurant with him on Saturday evening
4 it is possible to meet next week
5 Kate can't go, she has important business
6 Tom has a cold, we must call a doctor
7 you will take steak, fish with potato, a small piece of chicken and salad, tea and cake, please

Ask:

8 do you have any specials today?
9 have you known him long?
10 what do you want to drink?

Answers

1 Mnye pazvaneel gaspadeen Eevanof.
2 On kharoshiiy kleeyent nashiiy feermi.
3 F soobotoo vyecheeram mi s neem eedyom v reestaran.
4 Vazmozhno vstryeteetsa na slyedooshshyeeiy needyelee.
5 Kate nye mozhit eetee, oo neeyo vazhnaie deela.
6 Oo Toma prastooda, nada vizvat' vrachya.
7 Mnye, pazhaloosta beefshteks/riboo s kartoshkaiy/koosocheek kooritsi ee salat/chyaiy ee tort.
8 Oo vas yes't' seevodnya feermeeniee blyuda?
9 Vi yeevo davno znaeetee?
10 Shto vi khateetee peet'?

▶ Let's speak Russian – fast and fluently

Translate each section and check if it is correct. Then cover the answers and say the three or four sentences fast!

20 seconds per section for a silver star, 15 seconds for a gold star.

Some of the English is in 'Russian-speak' to help you.

Today called Barees.
He is our client, very good man.
He in Moscow for two days. By his important meeting.

Seevodnya pazvaneel Barees.
On nash kleeyent, ocheen' kharoshiiy cheelavyek.
On v Maskvye na dva dnya. Oo neevo vazhnaye fstryechya.

What shall we do tomorrow?
In centre, behind church is new restaurant.
By you have time?

Shto mi dyelaeem zaftra?
F tsentree, za tserkvayu yes't' noviy reestaran.
Oo vas yes't' vryemya?

I can't. By me ill wife, necessary it will be to call doctor.
I understand, it's a pity, but on next week?

Ya nee magoo. Oo meenya bal'na zhina, nada boodeet vizvat' vrachya.
Ya panimayu, ocheen' zhal', a na slyedooshsheeiy needyelee?

Now say all the sentences in Russian without stopping and starting. If you can do it in under one minute you are a fast and fluent winner!

But if you are not happy with your result – just try once more!

Test your progress

Translate the sentences into Russian.

1 I think the appointment is on Tuesday.
2 Today? No, I am sorry, that is not possible.
3 I must buy many presents.
4 Can('t) you help me, please? I want the number of the doctor.
5 Do(n't) you know where there is a good restaurant?
6 The church is very interesting, it seems.
7 We would like to travel on Monday evening, please.
8 Can I have the menu, please?
9 Excuse me, please, where are the papers?
10 Can one buy fruit here?
11 Do you know his new restaurant?
12 It was wonderful! Thank you very much for the pleasant evening.
13 Why is it necessary for you to see my credit card?
14 It was boring at the theatre on Monday.
15 You see the telephone upstairs by the exit, by the door.
16 We eat chicken or sausage... the fish is too expensive.
17 How does one say in Russian...?
18 Do(n't) you know where here bus? (where there is a bus here?)
19 My husband wants to go to Texas, but I would like to go to New York.
20 He does not know that the new restaurant is behind the church.

How did you get on? Another brilliant score on the Progress chart?

05

week five

How about 15 minutes on the train, tube or bus, 10 minutes on the way home and 30 minutes before switching on the television...?

Day one

- Read **On their way**.
- Listen to/Read **F pootee**.
- Read the **New words**. Learn 15 or more.

Day two

- Repeat the dialogue. Learn the harder **New words**.
- Cut out the **Flash words** to get stuck in.

Day three

- Test yourself to perfection on all the **New words**.
- Read and learn the **Good news grammar**.

Day four (the tough day)

- Listen to/Read **Learn by heart**.
- Cut out and learn the ten **Flash sentences**.

Day five

- Listen to/Read **Spot the keys**.
- Go over **Learn by heart**.

Day six

- Listen to/Read **Let's speak Russian**.
- Listen to/Read **Let's speak more Russian** (optional).
- Listen to/Read **Let's speak Russian – fast and fluently** (optional).
- Translate **Test your progress**.

Day seven

I bet you don't want a day off... but I insist!

day-by-day guide

On their way

Tom and Kate are travelling across Russia by train, bus and taxi. They talk to Olga, the ticket clerk, to Jim in the train and to Tatyana in the bus. (The English is in 'Russian-speak' to get you tuned in.)

(At the station)

Tom   Two tickets to Tver, please.

Olga   There and back?

Tom   There and how (what)? More slowly, please.

Olga   There... and... back.

Tom   To one end (single) only, please. When leaves train and from where?

Olga   At 9.45, from fifth platform.

Kate   More quickly (hurry), Tom, here are two places, for non-smokers. Oh, here is someone here smoking. Excuse me, in the train not possible to smoke. Because these seats are for non-smokers. Here to smoke is forbidden.

Jim   Sorry, I don't understand. I speak only English.

(At the bus stop)

Kate   On Sundays few buses. For us it is necessary to wait 20 minutes. Tom, here are my postcards and letter. Over there post box. And I want to take couple of photographs. River so beautiful in sun.

Tom   Kate, hurry. Are arriving two buses. Both yellow. First already full, the other is better.

(In the bus)

Tatyana Tickets it is necessary to punch!

Tom   Oh, yes, thank you. To museum it is far?

Tatyana This bus goes not to museum, but to hospital.

(In the taxi)

Tom   I very pleased. Taxi not bad and journey not too expensive costs.

Kate   To me does not please this car (I don't like), because it old and not clean... that's why cheaper. I hope that problems will not be.

┈┈➡ Page 66

▶ F pootee

Tom and Kate are travelling across Russia by train, bus and taxi. They talk to Olga, the ticket clerk, to Jim in the train and to Tatyana in the bus.

(Na vagzalee)

Tom	Dva beelyeta f Tvyer, pazhaloosta.
Olga	Tooda ee abratna?
Tom	Tooda ee kak? Pamyedleeneeye, pazhaloosta.
Olga	Tooda... ee... abratna.
Tom	Tol'ka, v adeen kanyets pazhaloosta. Kagda atkhodeet poeest ee atkooda?
Olga	V dyeveet' sorak pyat', ot pyataiy platformi.
Kate	Skaryeye, Tom, vot dva myesta, dlya neekooryashsheekh. Akh, vot kto-ta z'dyes' kooreet'. Eezveeneetee, f poeezdee neel'zya kooreet'. Patamoo shta etee meesta dlya neekooryashsheekh. Z'dyes' kooreet' zapreeshaeetsa.
Jim	Sorry, I don't understand. Ya gavaryu only English.

(Na astanofkee aftoboosa)

Kate	Pa vaskreesyen'yam mala aftoboosaf. Nam nada zhdat' dvatsat meenoot. Tom, vot maee atrkitkee ee pees'mo. Von tam pachtoviy yashsheek. A ya khachoo s'nyat' paroo fatagrafeeiy. Reeka tak kraseeva na sontsi.
Tom	Kate, skaryeye! Vot dva aftoboosa. Oba zholtiee. Pyervyiy oozhe polan, droogoiy loochshi.

(F avtoboosee)

Tatyana	Beelyeti nada prakampas'teeravat'!
Tom	Akh, da, kanyeshna. Do moozyeya daleeko?
Tatyana	Etat aftoboos yedeet nye v moozyeiy, a v bal'neetsoo.

(F taksee)

Tom	Ya ocheen' davoleen. Taksee neeplakhoye ee payestka nye sleeshkam doraga stoeet.
Kate	Mnye nye nraveetsa eta mashina, patamoo shta staraya ee nyecheestaya, vot pacheemoo deeshevlee. Ya nadyeyus', shto prablyem nye boodeet.

┈┈➡ Page 67

Tom   There was only this taxi. (*Later*) Where we? I don't see museum. On left petrol station and station of metro. On right school.

Kate   Here is plan of town. To museum, it seems, it is not far... to traffic lights, then right along main street. Why we so slowly travelling? Petrol has finished? Oil has finished? Taxi has broken down? Where my bag? Where mobile phone?

Tom   Kate, these questions lead me from mind (are driving me crazy). And it is raining. And why police travelling behind us?

▶ New words

poot'/pootee   *way, journey*
vagzal   (*railway*) *station*
beelyet/beelyety   *ticket/tickets*
dva beelyeta   *two tickets*
tooda   *to there*
abratna   *back/return*
pamyedleeneeye   *a little more slowly*
kanyets   *end, direction (one way)*
atkhadeet'/atkhodeet   *to leave/it leaves*
poeest/f poeezdee   *train/ in the train*
atkooda   *from where*
platforma/platformi   *platform*
skaryeye   *hurry*
neekooryashsheekh   *non-smokers*
kooreet'   *to smoke*
patamoo shta   *because*
zapreeshshaeetsa   *it is forbidden*
astanofka   *bus stop*
pa vaskreesyeneeyam   *on Sundays*
mala   *few, little*
zhdat'   *to wait*
pees'mo   *letter*
von tam   *over there*
pachtoviy yashsheek   *post box*

snyat'   *to take* (*of photographs*)
para/paroo   *pair, couple*
fatagrafiya/fatagrafeeiy   *photograph/photographs*
reeka   *river*
sontse   *sun*
oba   *both*
pyervyiy   *first*
polan   *full*
droogoiy   *other, another*
prakampasteeravat'   *to punch, clip*
moozyeiy/moozyeya   *museum*
(nee)daleeko   *it is* (*not*) *far,* (*not*) *distant*
etat/eta   *this*
bal'neetsa/bal'neetsoo   *hospital*
neeplakhoye   *not bad*
payestka   *journey*
mashina   *car*
staroye/staraya   *old*
neecheestaya   *not clean*
nadyeyatsa/nadyeyus'   *to hope/I hope*
taksee   *taxi*
eedyot dosht'   *it's raining*
veedeet'/veezhoo   *to see/I see*
beenzazaprafka *petrol station* (*colloquial*)
stantseeya meetro   *metro station*

Tom   Bila tol'ka eta taksee. *(Pozhe)* Gdye mi? Ya nee veezhoo moozyeiy. Nalyeva benzazaprafka ee stantseeya meetro. Naprava shkola.

Kate   Vot plan gorada. Da moozyeya, kazhitsa, needaleeko... da sveetafora, patom naprava po glavnaiy ooleetsi. Pacheemoo mi tak myedleena yedeem? Beenzeen koncheels'a? Masla koncheelas'? Taksee slamalas? Gdye maya soomka? Gdye sotaviy teeleefon?

Tom   Kate, etee vaprosee svodyat meenya s ooma. Ee eedyot dosht'. A pacheemoo meeleetsiya yedeet za namee?

shkola *school*	koncheelsa/koncheelas' *has finished*
plan gorada *plan of the town*	masla *oil*
sveetafor/sveetafora *traffic lights*	slamalas' *it has broken down*
glavnaiy ooleetsi *main street*	svodyat meenya s ooma *are driving me crazy*
myedleena *slowly*	meeleetsiya *police*
beenzeen *petrol*	

**TOTAL NEW WORDS: 60
...only 38 words to go!**

▶ Learn by heart

Someone crashed the car and someone else is getting suspicious!

Mashina tol'ka neemnoshka slamalas...

Zaftra nam mozhna smatryet' tenees? Oo meenya dva beelyeta na mach. Ya khachu veedeet' novykh ameereekanskeekh tineeseestaf.* Mozhna yekhat' tooda na meetro? Eelee loochshe na aftoboosee, patamoo shta on yedeet pryama na stadeeon.

Aftoboos? Meetro? Pacheemoo? Mnye nye nraveetsa garatskoiy transpart. Oo nas kraseevaya mashina.

Da, no... vcheera, kagda ya yekhala v gorat, ya nee ooveedeela sveetafor... no mashina tol'ka nyemnoshka slamalas...

*tineeseestaf: *tennis players*

▶ Good news grammar

1 *nraveetsa* – to like – or not like

Think how often you use this in English: *I like this – you don't like that – do you like...?*

In Russian you use 'nraveetsa', but it is a bit of a strange construction. Think of it as *something that is pleasing to you*:

I like the car –
    To me is pleasing the car.   Mnye nraveetsa mashina.
We don't like the car –
    To us is not pleasing the car.   Nam nye nraveetsa mashina.
Do you like to work? –
    To you is pleasing to work?   Vam nraveetsa rabotat'?

Once you get used to *is pleasing* it's quite simple really. Just remember 'nraveetsa'.

2 Saying the opposite – just add *nee*

This an easy way to double your vocabulary! As opposed to learning two words just use one and add 'nee':

Eta kraseeviy gorat.	*It is a beautiful town.*
Eta neekraseeviy gorat.	*It is an ugly (not beautiful) town.*
Magzeenee neeinteryesnyee.	*The shops are boring (not interesting).*

3 Another shortcut – can and can't

In such common phrases as *Can you hear...?* or *Can't you see...?* the Russians will leave out the *can* or *can't* altogether:

Ya slishoo yeevo.	*I can hear him.*
Vi nye veedeetee teeleeveezar?	*Can't you see the television?*

Makes it easier, doesn't it?

4 No more new grammar!

After this week there's no more new grammar. After all, you decided on **Instant Russian** because you wanted a starter kit – not a complicated textbook.

If you remember all the grammar notes, words and phrases in the book you'll have done very well indeed.

▶ Let's speak Russian

A ten-point warm-up: I give you an answer and you ask me a question as if you did not hear the words in CAPITAL LETTERS very well.

Example Veektar Z'DYES'. *Question* Gdye Veektar?

1 Sotaviy teeleefon V SOOMKEE.
2 SHKOLA von tam.
3 Poeest atkhodeet V TREE CHEESA.
4 TOM khocheet gavareet' s Bareesam Eevanaveecheem.
5 Beelyet tooda ee abratna stoeet 80 ROOBLYEIY.
6 Mnye nye nraveetsa mashina, PATAMOO SHTA ana staraya.
7 Vi yedeetee v Angleeyu … NA SAMALYOTEE.
8 Ya ooveedeel(a) SVEETAFOR.
9 DA, mnye nraveetsa gasteeneetsa.
10 Mnye nraveetsa MOOZYEIY.

Now answer starting with 'da':

11 Vi znaeetee noviy magazeen?
12 Vi yedeetee seechyas v bal'neetsoo?
13 Vam nraveetsa reeka?
14 Vi veedeetee astanofkoo aftoboosa?

Here are three things that you want to refer to. But you don't know what they are called in Russian. Explain them using the words you know:

15 a refrigerator
16 a holiday
17 a kennel

Answers

1 Gdye sotavyiy teeleefon?
2 Shto eta von tam?
3 Kagda atkhodeet poeest?
4 Kto khocheet gavereet' s Bareesam Eevanaveecheem?
5 Skol'ka stoeet beelyet tooda ee abratna?
6 Pacheemoo vam nye nraveetsa mashina?
7 Kak vi yedeete v Angleeyu?
8 Shto vi ooveedeelee?
9 Vam nraveetsa gasteeneetsa?
10 Shto vam nraveetsa?

11 Da, ya znayu noviy magazeen.
12 Da, ya yedoo seechyas v bal'neetsoo.
13 Da, mnye nraveetsa reeka.
14 Da, ya veezhoo astanofkoo aftoboosa.
15 Meesta, gdye kholadna, dlya malaka, myasa, sira.
16 Vryemya, kagda vi nye rabotaeetee.
17 Dom dlya sabakee, kagda mi v otpooskee.

▶ Let's speak more Russian

In your own words

This exercise will teach you to express yourself freely. Use only the words you have learned so far.

Tell me in your own words that...

1 the train leaves at 10.30 from the first platform
2 you hope there won't be any problems
3 on Saturdays there are few buses; it is necessary to wait for a long time
4 it is necessary to punch the tickets
5 the taxi is not expensive, but the car is old
6 you need two tickets to St Petersburg, there and back
7 you want to take a couple of photos, the church is so beautiful
8 you are driving along the main street to the railway station, then to the right
9 you can't see the taxi

Ask:

10 where are seats for non-smokers?

Answers

1 Poeesd atkhodeet v dyeseet' treetsat ot pyervaiy platformi.
2 Ya nadyeyus', shto prablyem nye boodeet.
3 Pa soobotam mala aftoboosaf, nada dolgo zhdat'.
4 Nada prakampasteeravat' beelyety.
5 Taksee stoeet nyedoraga, no mashina staraya.
6 Mnye dva beelyeta f Sankt-Peeteerboork, tooda i abratna.
7 Ya khachu snyat' paroo fatagrafeeiy, tserkaf tak kraseevaya.
8 Mi yedeem po glavnaiy ooleetsi do vagzala, patom naprava.
9 Ya nee veezhoo taksee.
10 Gdye meesta dlya neekooryashsheekh?

Translate each section and check if it is correct. Then cover the answers and say the three or four sentences fast!

25 seconds per section for a silver star, 20 seconds for a gold star.

Some of the English is in 'Russian-speak' to help you.

Ticket one way to Tver. How much?
More slowly, please. Yes, for me on train at 11.30.
Where platform number 5?

Beelyet v adeen kanyets f Tvyer'. Skol'ka?
Pamyedleeneeye, pazhaloosta. Da, mnye na poeest v adinatsat tritsat.
Gdye platforma nomeer pyat?

We need the post box.
Here are letter and photo.
More quickly, the bus is full again.
Other one it necessary to wait ten minutes.

Nam noozhin pachtoviy yashsheek.
Vot pees'mo ee fatagrafiya.
Skaryeye, aftoboos apyat' polan.
Droogoiy nada zhdat' dyeseet' meenoot.

Ten minutes wait, let's go on taxi.
To the metro, it seems, not far.
Along the main street, to the traffic light, then to the left.
Where my mobile phone?

Dyeseet' minoot zhdat', yedeem na taksee.
Do meetro, kazhitsa, nyedaleeko.
Po glavnaiy ooleetsi, do sveetafora, patom nalyeva.
Gdye moiy sotaviy teeleefon?

Now say all the sentences in Russian without stopping and starting. If you can do it in under one minute you are a fast and fluent winner!

But if you are not happy with your result – just try once more!

▶ Spot the keys

This time you are planning a trip in the country and want to have some idea what the weather will be like. This is what you could ask:

You   Eezveeneetee, pazhaloosta, vi nye mozhitee mnye skazat', kakaya zaftra boodeet pagoda?

Answer   *Eezveeneetee, ya nee znayu, no kagdayasmatryel* pragnoz pagodi po teeleeveezaroo, *skazalee, shto pagoda* myedleena *meenyaeetsa.* Zaftra *boodeet* kholadna – *voseem' gradoosaf, s neebal'shimoyetram ee* dosht boodeet k vyecheeroo.

She doesn't know, but according to the TV something slow is happening and it will be cold tomorrow, 8°C, with rain in the evening.

Test your progress

1   I don't like this bag. The other bag was better.
2   How much does (the) ticket cost – return?
3   What did you say? Slowly, please.
4   I know that in America petrol is cheaper.
5   In (the) underground it is forbidden to smoke.
6   I cannot wait, I have (an) appointment at 11 o'clock.
7   Is this (the) letter box? (A) yellow letter box?
8   Hello, we are 30 km from Novgorod. Is that (the) petrol station?
9   Which is cheaper? (The) bus or (the) metro?
10 Today it is very cold. I hope that it will rain.
11 The traffic light was red, not green. That's why they're both in hospital.
12 She was at (the) petrol station on Monday and Tuesday. The car drinks petrol!
13 Where here (is the) dry cleaner's? By me oil on T-shirt 'Armani'.
14 Our flat (is) behind (the) main street, by (the) bus stop.
15 We are by police (at the police station), because we do not know where my mobile phone (is).
16 It is necessary to buy (the) tickets now, because they cheaper.
17 I like your car. Was it very expensive?
18 Can you help us, please? Can one eat here by river?

If you know all your words you should score over 90%!

06

week six

This is your last week! Need I say more?

Day one

- Read **In the airport**.
- Listen to/Read **V aerapartoo**.
- Read the **New words**. There are only a handful!

Day two

- Read **V aerapartoo**. Learn all the **New words**.
- Work with the **Flash words** and **Flash sentences**.

Day three

- Test yourself on the **Flash sentences**.
- No more **Good news grammar**! Try the quiz instead.

Day four

- Listen to/Read and learn **Da sveedaneeya**.
- Listen to/Read **Spot the keys**.

Day five

- Listen to/Read **Let's speak Russian**.
- Read **Say it simply**.

Day six

- Listen to/Read **Let's speak more Russian** (optional).
- Listen to/Read **Let's speak Russian – fast and fluently** (optional).
- Your last **Test your progress**! Go for it!

Day seven

Congratulations!

You have successfully completed the course and can now speak

Instant Russian!

day-by-day guide

In the airport

Tom and Kate are on their way back to Birmingham. They are in the departure lounge of Moscow airport. (The English is in 'Russian-speak' to get you tuned in.)

Tom On Monday for us it is necessary will be to work. Terrible! I want (to go) to Italy or to Hawaii! No one in my firm knows where I (am).

Kate And in *my* firm? They know (the) number of telephone of my mother, and she knows the number of my mobile telephone...

Tom Yes, yes, I know. Well, perhaps at Christmas, (a) week in the snow or let's go on (a) ship to Madeira. But I want to buy (a) newspaper downstairs... Kate! There is Yuriy Zhivago!

Yuriy Hello! How are things? What you here are doing? This is my wife, Nancy. Already (the) end of your holiday? Well, how all went? (How did it go?)

Kate Splendidly! (wonderful). We much saw and too much ate. Now we well know Moscow, and Saint Petersburg...

Yuriy Next year for you it is necessary to (go to) Novgorod! Mrs Walker, my wife wants to buy a book for our computer. You (not) can help her (Could you help her at all?) Mr Walker, you have a newspaper. Give, please, (the) *Sport*. Then I invite you to (the) bar.

(*At the airport kiosk*)

Kate Here nothing suitable there is [not]. You also going to England?

Nancy No, we are going to Saint Petersburg. Mother of Yuriy lives there. Our children were by her for two weeks. By us (we have) boy and three girls. Tomorrow we are going to Novgorod on the train. It is cheaper.

Kate Your husband works in (a) bank?

Nancy Yes, his work (is) interesting, but money (is) not big. To our Lada already nine years (our Lada is already nine years old) and by us (we have) old, small flat. (In) this year much (we) have repaired. My parents and my girlfriend (are) in

⸻➡ Page 78

► V aerapartoo

Tom and Kate are on their way back to Birmingham. They are
in the departure lounge of Moscow airport.

Tom F paneedyelneek nam nada boodeet rabotat'. Oozhas!
Ya khachu v Italeeyu eelee na Gavaiyee! Neekto v mayeiy
feermee nye znaeet, gdye ya.

Kate A v mayeiy feermee? Anee znayut nomeer teeleefona
mayeiy mami, a ana znaeet nomeer mayevo sotavava
teeleefona.

Tom Da, da, znayu. Noo, mozhit bit' na Razhdeestvo,
needyelyu f snyegoo eelee payedeem na teeplakhodee
na Madyeiyroo. A ya khachu   koopeet' gazyetoo
vneezoo... Kate! Vot Yuriy Zhivaga!

Yuriy Zdrastvooiytee! Kak deela? Shto vi z'dyes' dyelaeetee?
Eta maya zhina, Nancy. Oozhe kanyets vashiva
otpooska? Noo, kak fsyo prashlo?

Kate Veeleekalyepna! Mi mnoga veedeelee ee sleeshkam
mnoga yelee. Seechyas mi kharasho znaeem ee Maskvoo
ee Sankt-Peeteerboork...

Yuriy F slyedooshsheem gadoo vam nada v Novgarat!
Gaspazha Walker, maya zhina khocheet koopeet'
kneegoo dlya nashiva kamp'yutira. Vi nye mozhitee yeiy
pamoch'? Gaspadeen Walker, oo vas gazyeta. Daiytee,
pazhaloosta, *Sport*. Patom preeglashayu vas v bar.

(*V aerapartoo, oo keeooska*)

Kate Z'dyes' neecheevo patkhadyashsheeva nyet. Vi tozhe
yedeetee v Angleeyu?

Nancy Nyet, mi yedeem f Sankt-Peeteerboork. Mama Yuriiya
zhivyot tam. Nashi dyetee bilee oo neeyo dvye needyelee.
Oo nas mal'cheek ee tree dyevachkee. Zaftra mi yedeem
v Novgarat na poeezdee. Eta deeshevlee.

Kate Vash moosh rabotaeet v bankee?

Nancy Da, yeevo rabota eenteeryesnaya, no dyen'gee
nyebal'shiee. Nasheiy Ladee oozhe dyeveet' lyet ee oo
nas staraya, maleen'kaya kvarteera. V etam gadoo
mnoga   atreemanteeravalee.   Maee radeeteelee ee
padrooga f S-SHA ee mi chyasta peeshim pees'ma.

······► Page 79

(the) USA and we often write letters. I would like (to go) to America, but too expensive costs.

Kate But by you (you have) (a) beautiful house in Greece.

Nancy (A) house in Greece? I never [not] was in Greece (I have never been to Greece). When by us (we have) (a) holiday, we go to friend('s), at Cheelyabeensk.

Tom Kate, hurry, for us it is time (to go). What said Mrs Zhivago?

Kate Wait, Tom, wait!

▶ New words

Italeeya/v Italeeyu *Italy/to Italy*
Gavaiyee *Hawaii*
mami/mama *mother*
Razhdeestvo *Christmas*
snyek/sneegoo *snow*
payedeem *let's go*
teeplakhot/teeplakhodee *ship*
Madyeiyra/Madyeiyroo *Madeira*
vneezoo *downstairs*
kak deela? *how are things?*
prashlo *it went by, passed*
veeleekalyepna *splendid(ly), great, wonderful(ly)*
yelee *we/they ate*
f slyedooshshee/etam gadoo *next/this year*
kneega *book*
daiytee *give!*
preeglashat'/preeglashayu *to invite/I invite*
bar *bar*
neecheevo *nothing*

patkhadyashsheeiy/patkhadyashsheeva *suitable*
zhivyot *lives*
dyetee *children*
dvye (f) *two*
mal'cheek *boy*
dyevachka/dyevachkee *(little) girl/girls*
deeshyevlee *cheaper*
moosh *husband*
Lada/Ladoo *Lada*
lyet *of years*
maleen'keeiy/maleen'kaya *small*
S-SHA *USA*
peeshim *we write*
chyasta *often*
pees'ma *letters*
neekagda nee *never*
droog/droogoo *friend*
para *it is time (to go)*
padazhdee! *wait!*

TOTAL NEW WORDS: 38
TOTAL RUSSIAN WORDS LEARNED: 381
EXTRA WORDS: 80

GRAND TOTAL: 461

Ya **o**cheen' khat**y**ela bi v Am**y**er**ee**koo, no sl**ee**shkam d**o**raga st**o**eet.

Kate   No oo vas kras**ee**vyiy dom v Gr**y**etsi-ee.

Nancy   Dom v Gr**y**etsi-ee? Ya n**ee**kagd**a** nee bil**a** v Gr**y**etsi-ee. Kagd**a** oo nas **o**tpoosk, mi **y**ed**ee**m k dr**oo**goo f Cheel**y**ab**ee**nsk.

Tom   Kate! Skar**y**eye, nam par**a**! Shto skaz**a**la gaspazh**a** Zhiv**a**ga?

Kate   Pad**a**zhd**ee**, Tom, pad**a**zhd**ee**!

▶ Learn by heart

This is your last dialogue to **Learn by heart**. Give it your best! You now have six prize-winning party pieces, and a large store of everyday sayings which will be very useful.

Da svee**dan**ee**ya!**

Kate   Bar**ee**s Vad**ee**maveech, gavar**ee**t Kate Walker, a ya v aerapart**oo** v Maskv**ye**.
Da, **oo**zhe kan**y**ets n**a**shiva **o**tpooska ee n**a**sheekh d**y**en**ee**k t**o**zhe!
Spas**ee**ba balsh**o**ye za **o**cheen' pre**ey**atniiy v**y**echeer! Tom kh**o**cheet gavar**ee**t' s v**a**mee.

Tom   Zdrastv**oo**iytee, Bar**ee**s Vad**ee**maveech... Kak? Vi khat**ee**tee koop**ee**t' **o**ba?
Oo m**ay**eiy f**ee**rmi yes't' vash e-mail? Veel**ee**kal**y**epna. Spas**ee**ba balsh**o**ye!
F sl**ye**d**oo**shsheem gad**oo**?... Kate kh**o**cheet v Ital**ee**yu, no mn**ye** nrav**ee**tsa Ras**ee**ya.*
S Edith Palmer? Akh, B**o**zhe moiy, nyet, nyet! Nash samal**yo**t zhd**yo**t**... Noo... Da sv**ee**dan**ee**ya!

---

*Ras**ee**ya: *Russia*
zhdyo**t: *is waiting*

Good news grammar

There's no more grammar this week, just a couple of interesting points.

1 Double negative

The Russians love to say nyet so they sometimes say it twice!

Neekto nye znaeet, gdye ya.   *No one not knows where I am.*
Ya neekagda nye bila   *I never not was in Greece.*
  v Gryetsi-ee.

2 Surnames

Yuriy Baranav... and his wife, **Mrs Baranava**. In Russian, a man's surname usually ends in a consonant and a woman's in the letter 'a' (thus **Anna Karyeneena's** husband's surname was **Karyeneen**).

3 Quiz

And now for some light relief: the end of course quiz!

No marks for this one – just a pat on the back!

1 In which city would you find the Kryeml'?
  a Sankt-Peeteerboork   **c** Yalta
  b Maskva   **d** Vladeevastok

2 How would you say 12 o'clock in Russian?
  a dva cheesa   **c** dveenatsat' cheesof
  b dvatsat' cheesof

3 How would you greet someone if you met them in the evening?
  a dobraye **ootra**   **c** da sveedaneeya
  b dobriiy dyen'   **d** dobriiy vyecheer

4 If you were a vegetarian, which of these would you not eat?
  a myasa   **c** tort
  b frookti   **d** kartoshka

5 When do you celebrate Christmas in Russia?
  a 24 deekabrya   **c** 31 deekabrya
  b 25 deekabrya   **d** 6 yeenvarya

6 If you wanted to apologize, what would you say?
  a kharasho   **c** oozhasna
  b eezveeneetee   **d** kanyeshna

7 When does *Dyet Maros* (the Russian version of Father Christmas) bring presents?
  a 24 deekabrya   **c** 31 deekabrya
  b 25 deekabrya   **d** 6 yeenvarya

8 What does 'shto vam' mean?
   a Where are you?   c Where do you work?
   b What would you like?

9 How do you say in Russian *I understand*?
   a ya paneemayu   c ya khachu
   b ya znayu   d ya magoo

10 What do Russians say when they really don't approve of
    what you want to do?
    a tak mozhna   c tak nada
    b tak neel'**zya**   d tak nye gadeetsa

You'll find the answers on page 91.

▶ Spot the keys

Here's a final practice round. If you have the recording, close the
book now. Find the key words and try to get the gist of it. Then
check on page 91.

This is what you might ask a taxi driver:

You   Skol'ka meenoot do aeraporta ee skol'ka stoeet?
Answer   *Eta zaveeseet ot tavo, kagda vi yedeetee. Abichna*
             payestha dleetsa dvatsat' meenoot, no yeslee vi
             khateetee yekhat' f chyasee peek ee veez'dee prophee,
             payestha mozhit dleetsa sorak pyat ... asobeenna
             pa pyatneetsam, kagda khoozhe fseevo. Skol'ka
             stoeet? Abichna ot treetsatee do peeteedeeseetee rooblyeiy.

Say it simply

1 You are staying in a hotel in Russia. The television and the
shower are both broken. Report it – you want to use both!

2 You are at the airport, about to catch your flight home when
you realize that you have left a bag behind in the room of your
hotel. You phone the hotel reception and ask for it to be sent on
to you.

What would you say in these two cases? Say it then write it
down. Then see the two examples on page 91. Yours can be
different and even simpler, based solely on your **Instant**
vocabulary. Give it a go!

◗ Let's speak Russian

Here's a quick warm-up. Answer the questions using the words in brackets.

1 On koopeel dom v Marbella? (da, paneedyel'neek)
2 Skol'ka lyet vi rabotalee v bankee? (pyat)
3 Kagda vi gavareelee s vashiiy feermaiy? (fcheera)
4 Pacheemoo vam nada atryemanteeravat' vashoo mashinoo? (patamoo shta, ana staraya)
5 On bil snachala v gasteeneetsi? (nyet, f kvarteeree)

Now practise your verbs with 'nada', 'neelzya' and 'para':

6 Oozhas! Kvarteera ocheen' staraya… (You mustn't buy it).
7 Skaryeye! Oozhe dyeveet' cheesof… (It's time for us to go).
8 … (You must mend the television), yeslee on nee rabotaeet.

Finish off the sentences, using phrases which start with 'shto' and 'patamoo shta':

9 Maya padrooga skazala… (that already end of holiday).
10 Eeshshyo ana skazala… (that she really likes Moscow).
11 Maya zhina khocheet skazat'… (that she has (a) cold).
12 Moiy moosh gavareet, shto on nee mozhit f tyatr… (because he is working).
13 Ol'ga tozhe ne mozhit f tyatr… (because she is on holiday).
14 Moiy droog gavareet… (that she is very beautiful).
15 On gavareet tozhe… (that he wants her telephone number).

Answers

1 Da, on koopeel dom v Marbella f paneedyel'neek.
2 Ya rabotal/rabotala v bankee pyat lyet.
3 Ya gavareel/gavareela s mayeiy feermaiy fcheera.
4 Nam nada atreemanteeravat' mashinoo, patamoo shta ana staraya.
5 Nyet, snachala on bil f kvarteeree.
6 Oozhas! Kvarteera ocheen' staraya. Vam nee nada yeyo.
7 Skaryeye! Oozhe dyeveet cheesof. Nam para eetee.
8 Vam nada atreemanteeravat' teeleeveezar, yeslee on nee rabotaeet.
9 Maya padrooga skazala, shto oozhe kanyets otpooska.

10 Eeshshyo ana skazala, shto yeiy ocheen' nraveetsa Maskva.
11 Maya zhina khoch'eet skazat', shto oo neeyo prastooda.
12 Moiy moosh gavareet, shto on nee mozhit v tyatr, patamoo shta on rabotayet.
13 Ol'ga tozhe ne mozhit f tyatr, patamoo shta ana v otpooskye.
14 Moiy droog gavareet, shto ana ocheen' kraseevaya.
15 On gavareet tozhe, shto on khocheet yeeyo nomeer teeleefona.

▶ Let's speak more Russian

In your own words

This exercise will teach you to express yourself freely. Use only the words you have learned so far.

Tell me in your own words that...

1 tomorrow is the end of your holiday
2 nobody knows where you have been
3 next year you are going on a ship to Saint-Petersburg
4 your mother knows the number of your mobile phone
5 you are going to Novgorod on the train; it is cheaper
6 now you know Tver well
7 at Christmas you are going to your friend in England
8 his wife works in Moscow
9 your children were with (by) him in the flat
10 you like the restaurant

Answers

1 Zaftra kanyets nashiva otpooska.
2 Neekto nye znaeet, gdye mi bilee.
3 V slyedooyshsheem gadoo mi payedeem na teeplakhodee f Sankt-Peeteerboork.
4 Mama znaeet nomeer nashiva sotavava teeleefona.
5 Mi yedeem v Novgarat na poeezdee, tak deeshevlee.
6 Seechas mi kharasho znaeem Tvyer.
7 Na Razhdeestvo mi payedeem g droogoo v Angleeyu.
8 Yeevo zhina rabotaeet v Maskvye.
9 Nashi dyetee bilee oo neevo v kvarteeree.
10 Mnye nraveetsa reestaran.

▶ Let's speak Russian – fast and fluently

Translate each section and check if it is correct. Then cover the answers and say the three or four sentences fast!

30 seconds for a silver star, 20 seconds for a gold star.

I want to (go to) Hawaii for several days.
We have never been in Moscow.
In my firm they know the number of my mobile phone.

Ya khachu na Gavaiyee na nyeskal'ka dnyeiy.
Mi neekagda nye bilee v Maskvye.
V mayeiy feermee znayut nomeer sotavava teelefona.

The girlfriend invites me to Greece on the boat.
It is interesting, but expensive costs. Cheaper to buy ticket to Sochi.
There by us beautiful house.

Padrooga preeglashaeet meenya v Gryetsiyu na teeplakhodee.
Eta eenteeryesna, no doraga stoeet. Deeshevlee koopeet' beelyet f Sochee.
Tam oo nas kraseeviy dom.

What are you doing here? My husband wants to buy computer.
You can't us help? Here nothing suitable not.
Downstairs can buy cheaper.

Shto vi z'dyes' dyelaeetee? Moiy moosh khocheet koopeet' kamp'yutir.
Vi nye mozhitee nam pamoch'? Z'dyes' neecheevo padhadyashsheeva nyet.
Vneezoo mozhna koopeet' deeshevlee.

Now say all the sentences in Russian without stopping and starting. If you can do it in under one minute you are a fast and fluent winner!

But if you are not happy with your result – just try once more!

Test your progress

A lot of **Instant** verbs have been crammed into this. But don't panic – it looks worse than it is. Go for it – you'll do brilliantly*!*

1 I like writing letters because I have (a) new computer.
2 How are you? You have (a) problem? To help you? Can I help you?
3 Excuse me, do you have the number of (her) mobile?
4 I like (the) Crimea (Krim). It is never cold there.
5 The other case is in (the) bus. Have you got (the) brown bag?
6 Where will you be at Christmas?
7 Who wants fish and who wants meat?
8 He has my telephone number. He often rings me.
9 Quickly! Where is (the) ticket? The train is coming!
10 Don't you know that (the) airport is always open?
11 My holiday is very important. I want (to go) to Italy.
12 Have you seen Olga in the newspaper? Without (her) husband?
13 Your mother is very pleasant. Her walnut cake is delicious!
14 We must work. We have three boys and one girl. Very expensive costs!
15 Excuse me, where is it possible to repair (the) car?
16 I know him. He always goes shopping with (his) dog.
17 Who said it is impossible (one cannot) here to smoke?
18 We are travelling to (the) airport by taxi, then to Dallas by 'plane.
19 I would like to speak to (the) waiter. Where is (the) bill?
20 I am sorry, but this is the end of **Instant Russian**.

Check your answers on page 90. Then enter your final excellent score on the Progress chart and write out your certificate!

answers

How to score

From a total of 100%

- Subtract 1% for each wrong or missing word.
- Subtract 1% for the wrong form of the verb, like **yed**eem when it should be **yed**oo.
- Subtract 1% for mixing up the pronouns such as vi, vam, vamee.

There are no penalties for:

- Wrong or different ending of the word, e.g. kamp'**yut**ir – kamp'**yut**ira. In a very few cases you will not already have met the correct word ending that you see in the answer. As long as you have the right word, you're doing fine and will be understood. Remember, near enough is good enough.
- Picking the wrong 'version' of the word, e.g. noviy – novim.
- Picking the wrong word where there are two of similar meaning, e.g. 'no' and 'a'.
- Wrong spelling, as long as you can say the word! e.g. ee**y**un – i**y**oon.
- Different word order.

For each test, correct your mistakes. Then read the corrected answers out loud twice.

**100% LESS YOUR PENALTIES WILL GIVE
YOU YOUR WEEKLY SCORE**

Week 1

Test your progress

1 Meenya zavoot Frank Lukas.
2 Zdrastvooitee, mi – Veektar ee Ol'ga.
3 Ya tozhe eez Omska.
4 V aktyabrye ya bil/bila v Maskvye.
5 Mi bilee tree goda v Amyereekee.
6 Londan stoeet doraga.
7 Eezveeneetee, pazhaloosta, gdye vi rabotaeetee?
8 Vi rabotaeete v Manchyes'teeree?
9 Vi Veektar Eezmaiylaf ees Tomska?
10 Kvarteera v Novgaradee ocheen' bal'shaya.
11 Meenootachkoo, pazhaloosta, oo meenya bol'shi dyeneek.
12 Tam yes't' teeleefon? Nyet, k sazhilyeneeyu.
13 Ya v Yaltee bees sina.
14 Feerma bal'shaya?
15 Meerseedes doraga stoeet?
16 V apryelee Londan ocheen' kraseeviiy.
17 Oo neevo f tooragyentstvee padrooga.
18 K sazhilyeneeyu rabota ocheen' skoochnaya.
19 Rabota ocheen' kharoshaya, no otpoosk loochshe.
20 Maya doch vseegda zvaneet.

YOUR SCORE: _____ %

Week 2

Test your progress

1 Ya p'yu mnoga shampanskava.
2 Skol'ka stoeet zaftrak, pazhaloosta.
3 Z'dyes' yes't' tooragyenstva?
4 Oo vas yes't' stol? F syem peetnatsat'?
5 Ya khachu peet' kofee.
6 Moiy otpoosk va Flareedee bil loochshe.
7 Gdye kharoshaya gasteeneetsa?
8 Telefoniy shshyot, pazhaloosta.
9 Mi bilee f Sankt-Peeteerboorgee v maee.
10 Moiy dom sleeshkam bal'shoiy.
11 F katoram chyasoo vi v Maskvoo zaftra?
12 Ya tam s vos'mee do peetee.
13 Eezveeneetee, pazhaloosta. Gdye tooalyety, pryama?

14 Mi khateem yekhat' v Osla v yeenvarye, no sleeshkam kholadna.
15 Eta stoeet bol'shi dyeneek?
16 Zaftra, gdye vi v dyeseet' treetsat?
17 Oozhasna. Nomeer ocheen' doraga stoeet.
18 Z'dyes' mozhna peet' kofee seechyas? Oo vas yes't' meesta?
19 Oo nas maleenkieeiy dom v Amyereekee, no on ocheen' doraga stoeet.
20 Da sveedaneeya, mi yedeem v Yaltoo.

YOUR SCORE: _____ %

Week 3

Test your progress

1 Gdye pradavyets?
2 Gdye mozhna koopeet' bootirbrodi?
3 Kagda vam nada v Angleeyu seevodnya? F syem' cheesof?
4 Mi ooveedeelee eta vcheera po teeleeveezaroo.
5 Seechyas magazeeni atkriti, kazhitsa.
6 Z'dyes' yes't' ooneeveermak eelee soopeermarkeet?
7 Eezveeneetee, vi tozhe eedyotee na pochtoo?
8 Gdye vi koopeelee angleeskooyu gazyetoo?
9 Vi khateetye kofee eelee chyaiy?
10 Seevodnya pagoda plakhaya. Neel'zya v Novgarat.
11 Eta fsyo? Eta bila needoraga.
12 Markee stoeelee peetnatsat' roobleiy.
13 Mi preeneemaeem kreedeetniee kartochkee.
14 Treesta gram sira sleeshkam mnoga? Nyet, nyet prablyem.
15 Yes't' novaya kheemcheestka bleeska atsyuda.
16 Oo vas yes't' pakyeteek dlya maeiy foodbolkee, pazhaloosta?
17 Ya z'dyes' ooveedeela aptyekoo, kazhitsa.
18 Bozhe moiy! Aftoboos nee rabotaeet ee Meerseedes tozhe nee rabotaeet!
19 Vi ooveedeelee foodbolkoo? Gdye vi koopeelee yeeyo?
20 Peetsot rooblyeiy, no oo meenya tolka dolari.

YOUR SCORE: _____ %

Week 4

Test your progress

1 Ya doomayu, shto fstryechya va ftorneek.
2 Seevodnya? Nyet, eezveeneetee, eta neevazmozhna.
3 Mnye nada koopeet' mnoga padarkaf.
4 Vi nye mozhite mnye pamoch', pazhaloosta? Ya khachu nomeer vrachya.
5 Vi nye znaeete, gdye yes't' kharoshiy reestaran?
6 Tserkaf' ocheen' eentyeryesnaya, kazhitsa.
7 Mi khatyelee bi yekhat' f paneedyel'neek vyecheeram pazhaloosta.
8 Mozhna meenyu, pazhaloosta?
9 Eezveeneetee, pazhaloosta, gdye boomagee?
10 Z'dyes' mozhna koopeet' frookti?
11 Vi znaeete yeevo noviy reestaran?
12 Eta bila preekrasna. Spaseeba balshoye za ocheen' preeyatniy vyecheer.
13 Pacheemoo vam nada veedeet' mayu kreedeetnooyu kartachkoo?
14 Bila skooshna f tyatree f paneedyel'neek.
15 Vi veedeetee teeleefon naveerkhoo, okala vikhada, okala dvyeree.
16 Mi yedeem kooreetsoo eelee kalbasoo... riba sleeshkam doraga stoeet.
17 Kak pa-roosskee...?
18 Vi nee znaeetee, gdye z'dyes' aftoboos?
19 Moiy moosh khocheet yekhat' f Teekhas, a ya khatyela bi yekhat' v N'yu York.
20 On nee znaeet, shto noviy reestaran za tserkav'yu.

YOUR SCORE: _____ %

Week 5

Test your progress

1 Mnye nee nraveetsa eta soomka. Droogaya soomka bila loochshe.
2 Skol'ka stoeet beelyet – tooda ee abratna?
3 Shto vi skazalee? Pamyedleeneeye, pazhaloosta.
4 Ya znayu, shto v Amyereekee beenzeen deeshevlee.
5 V meetro kooreet' zapreeshshaeetsa.
6 Ya nye magoo zhdat'. Oo meenya fstryechya v adeenatsat' cheesof.

7 Eta pachtoviy **ya**shsheek? Zholtiy **ya**shsheek?
8 Allo, mi f treetsat**ee** keelam**ye**trakh ot N**o**vgarada. **E**ta benzazapraf**ka**?
9 Shto deeshevl**ee**? Aft**o**boos **ee**l**ee** meetr**o**?
10 Seev**o**dnya **o**cheen' kh**o**ladna. Nad**ye**yus, b**oo**deet dosht.
11 Sveetaf**or** bil krasn**yi**y, nee zeel**yo**nyiy. Vot pacheem**oo** an**ee** **o**ba v baln**ee**tsi.
12 An**a** bil**a** na benzazaprafk**oi**y f paneed**ye**l'neek ee va ft**or**neek. Mashina p'yot beenz**ee**n!
13 Gdye z'des' kheemch**ee**stka? Oo meen**ya** m**a**sla na foodb**o**lkee 'Arm**a**nee'.
14 N**a**sha kvart**ee**ra za gl**a**vnaiy **oo**leetseiy, oo (*or* **o**kala) astan**o**fkee aft**o**boosa.
15 Mi v meel**ee**tsi-ee, patam**oo** shta mi nee zn**a**eem, gdye moiy s**o**taviy teel**ee**f**o**n.
16 N**a**da koop**ee**t' beel**ye**ti seech**ya**s, patam**oo** shta an**ee** deeshevl**ee**.
17 M**nye** nrav**ee**tsa v**a**sha mashina. An**a** **o**cheen' d**o**raga st**o**eela?
18 Vi nee m**o**zhitee nam pam**o**ch'? M**o**zhna z'dyes' yes't' **o**kala reek**ee**?

YOUR SCORE: _____ %

Week 6

Quiz

1b 2c 3d 4a 5d 6b 7c 8b 9a 10b/d

Spot the keys

Depends when you travel. Usually 20 minutes, but at rush hour when traffic jams everywhere, journey might last 45 minutes. Cost usually between 30 and 50 roubles.

Say it simply

1 Eezveen**ee**tee, pazhal**oo**sta, ya v n**o**meere 222. Tam teeleev**ee**zar nee rab**o**taeet ee doosh nee rab**o**taeet. Pazhal**oo**sta, eekh n**a**da atreemant**ee**ravat'. Ya nad**ye**yus, shto vi m**o**zhitee mnye pam**o**ch'!
2 Zdr**a**stvooiytee. Gav**a**r**ee**t Kate Green. Ya bil**a** v v**a**sheiy gast**ee**neetse, v n**o**meer**ee**... K sazhil**ye**neeyu ya **oo**zh**e** v aerapart**oo**, a m**a**ya s**oo**mka v n**o**meer**ee**. Pazhal**oo**sta, m**a**yu

soomkoo nada v Angleeyu. Gasteeneetsa znaeet, gdye ya zhivoo. Spaseeba bal'shoye.

Test your progress

1 Mnye nraveetsa peesat' pees'ma, patamoo shta oo meenya noviiy kamp'yutir.
2 Kak deela? Oo vas prablyema? Vam pamoch'?
3 Eezveeneetee, oo vas yes't' nomeer yeeyo sotavava teeleefona?
4 Mnye nraveetsa Krim. Tam neekagda nee kholadna.
5 Droogoiy cheemadan v aftoboosee. Oo vas kareechneevaya soomka?
6 Gdye vi boodeetee na Razhdeestvo?
7 Kto khocheet riboo ee kto khocheet myasa?
8 Oo neevo moiy nomeer teeleefona. On chyasta zvaneet mnye.
9 Skaryeye! Gdye beelyet? Poeest eedyot!
10 Vi nee znaeete, shto aeraport vseegda atkrit?
11 Moiy otpoosk ocheen' vazhniy. Ya khachu v Italeeyu.
12 Vi veedeelee Ol'goo v gazyetee? Beez moozha?
13 Vasha mama ocheen' preeyatnaya. Yeeyo aryekhaviy tort ocheen' fkoosniy!
14 Nam nada rabotat'. Oo nas tree mal'cheeka ee adna dyevachka. Ocheen' doraga stoeet!
15 Eezveeneetee, gdye mozhna atreemanteeravat' mashinoo?
16 Mi yeevo znaeem. On vseegda dyelaeet pakoopkee s sabakaiy.
17 Kto skazal, shto z'dyes' neel'zya kooreet'?
18 Mi yedeem v aeraport na taksee, patom v Dallas na samalyotee.
19 Ya khachu gavareet' s afeetseeantam. Gdye shshyot?
20 Eezveeneetee, no eta kanyets **Instant Russian**.

YOUR SCORE: _____ %

how to use the flash cards

The **Flash cards** have been voted the best part of this course! Learning words and sentences can be tedious, but with flash cards it's quick and good fun.

This is what you do:

When the **Day-by-day guide** tells you to use the cards, cut them out. There are 22 **Flash words** and 10 **Flash sentences** for each week. Each card has a little number on it telling you to which week it belongs, so you won't cut out too many cards at a time or muddle them up later on.

First, try to learn the words and sentences by looking at both sides of the cards. Then, when you have a rough idea, start testing yourself. That's the fun bit. Look at the English, say the Russian, and then check. Make a pile each for the 'correct', 'wrong' and 'don't know' ones. When all the cards are used up, start again with the 'wrong' pile and try to whittle it down until you get all of them right. You can also play it 'backwards' by starting with the Russian face-up.

Keep the cards in a little box or put an elastic band around them. Take them with you on the bus, the train, to the hairdresser's or the dentist's. If you find the paper too flimsy, photocopy the words and sentences onto card before cutting them up. You could also buy some plain card and stick them on or simply copy them out.

The 22 **Flash words** for each week are there to start you off. Convert the rest of the **New words** to **Flash words**, too. It's well worth it!

FLASH CARDS for Instant LEARNING:
DON'T LOSE THEM – USE THEM!

eezvee-**nee**tee	pazh**a**loosta
oo nas	da
mi	nyet
ya	**ye**doo
vi	rab**o**tayu
gdye	rab**o**ta

please [1]	excuse me [1]
yes [1]	by us (we have) [1]
no [1]	we [1]
I go (travel) [1]	I [1]
I work [1]	you [1]
work, job [1]	where [1]

khar**o**shiy/ khar**o**shaya [1]	d**ye**neek [1]
oo meen**ya** [1]	**e**ta [1]
bank банк [1]	v **o**tpooskee [1]
dom [1]	vseegd**a** [1]
g**o**rat [1]	s**o**taviy teeleef**o**n [1]
n**a**da [2]	sk**o**l'ka [2]

money [1]	good [1]
it is [1]	I have [1]
on holiday [1]	bank [1]
always [1]	house [1]
mobile phone [1]	town [1]
how much/ how many [2]	it is necessary [2]

2 roobl**yeiy**	2 na cheelav**ye**ka
2 kreed**ee**tniee k**ar**tachkee	2 z**a**ftrak
2 mi khat**ee**m	2 m**o**zhna
2 chyaiy	2 z'dyes'
2 bl**ee**ska	2 napr**a**va
2 vi, vas	2 fsyo

per person **2**	roubles **2**
breakfast **2**	credit cards **2**
it is possible **2**	we want **2**
here **2**	tea **2**
on the right **2**	near **2**
all, everything **2**	you **2**

oozh**a**sniiy [2]	m**a**leen'keeiy [2]
tooal**ye**ti [2] M (gents) Ж (ladies)	shshyot [2]
z**a**ftra [2]	pr**ya**ma [2]
stol [2]	mn**o**ga [2]
na [3]	aft**o**boos(ee) [3]
plakh**a**ya [3]	p**o**chta/ [3] p**o**chtoo почта

small [2]	terrible [2]
bill [2]	toilets [2]
straight on [2]	tomorrow [2]
much, many [2]	table [2]
bus [3]	on, by [3]
post office [3]	bad [3]

3	**3**
m**a**rkee	neel'z**ya**
3	**3**
s**oo**mka	ooneeveer-m**a**g
3	**3**
magaz**ee**n/ee	atkr**i**t(i)
3	**3**
nyet prabl**ye**m	koop**ee**t'
3	**3**
shto	neemn**o**shka
3	**3**
gaz**ye**ta	vot

it's not possible **3**	stamps **3**
department store **3**	bag **3**
open **3**	shop/s **3**
to buy **3**	no problem! **3**
a little **3**	what/that **3**
here is, here are **3**	newspaper **3**

3 eed**yo**t	3 pag**o**da
3 pak**oo**pkee	3 pad**ar**kee
3 preekr**a**snaya	3 kh**o**ladna
4 kto-ta	4 pachem**oo**
4 n**o**meer	4 klee**ye**nt
4 kharash**o**	4 v**a**zhniee

3	3
weather	(he, she, it, goes)
3	**3**
presents	shopping
3	**3**
cold	splendid
4	**4**
why	someone
4	**4**
client	number
4	**4**
important	good, well

4 kan**ye**shna	4 eentee-**rye**sna
4 kagd**a**	4 spas**ee**ba balsh**oiy**
4 prast**oo**da	4 vrach/ vrach**ya**
4 r**i**ba/r**i**boo	4 beefsht**e**ks
4 p**ee**va	4 stak**a**n
4 vad**a**/vad**i**	4 neekt**o**

it is interesting **4**

of course **4**

thank you very much **4**

when **4**

doctor **4**

cold **4**

steak **4**

fish **4**

glass **4**

beer **4**

no one **4**

water **4**

4	4
naveerkh**oo**	**o**kala

4	4
k**oo**reetsa	p**o**zna

5	5
vagz**a**l вокзал	abr**a**tna

5	5
p**o**eest	zapree- shsh**a**eetsa

5	5
m**a**la	pees'm**o**

5	5
pacht**o**viy y**a**shsheek	**o**ba

4 near, by	**4** upstairs
4 it is late	**4** chicken
5 back/return	**5** (railway) station
5 it is forbidden	**5** train
5 letter	**5** few, little
5 both	**5** post box

pye**rvyiy** 5	p**o**lan 5
droog**oiy** 5	**e**tat/**e**ta 5
mash**i**na 5	st**a**roye/ st**a**raya 5
astan**o**fka aft**o**boosa остановка 5	gl**a**vnaiy **oo**leetsi 5
m**ye**dleena 5	meel**ee**tsiya 5
skar**ye**ye! 5	eed**yo**t dosht' 5

5	5
full	first
5 this	**5** other, another
5 old	**5** car
5 main street	**5** bus stop
5 police	**5** slowly
5 it's raining	**5** hurry!

5 shk**o**la	5 bal'n**ee**tsa
6 Razhdeestv**o**	6 snyek/ sneeg**oo**
6 pa**ye**deem	6 teeplakh**o**t
6 S-SHA	6 veeleekal- **ye**pna
6 ch**ya**sta	6 vneez**oo**
6 aerap**o**rt аэропорт	6 neecheev**o**

5 hospital	5 school
6 snow	6 Christmas
6 ship	6 let's go
6 great, wonderful	6 USA
6 downstairs	6 often
6 nothing	6 airport

6 d**ye**tee	**6** m**a**l'cheek
6 d**ye**vachka	**6** kn**ee**ga
6 neekagd**a** nee	**6** rad**ee**teelee
6 droog/ dr**oo**goo	**6** par**a**
6 kak deel**a**?	**6** padazhd**ee**!
6 sl**ye**doosh- shee	**6** moosh

boy **6**	children **6**
book **6**	(little) girl **6**
parents **6**	never **6**
it's time (to go) **6**	friend **6**
wait! **6**	how's things? **6**
husband **6**	next **6**

Meen**ya** zav**oo**t John. 1

Ya bil v N**o**vgaradee. 1

pa b**ee**znisoo 1

Oo meen**ya** kvart**ee**ra. 1

Ya rab**o**tayu v L**o**ndanee. 1

Oo nas s**i**n ee doch. 1

Gdye vi rab**o**taeetee? 1

Mi **ye**deem v Maskv**oo**. 1

Rab**o**ta khar**o**shaya. 1

Vi v **o**tpooskee? 1

My name is John.

1

I was in Novgorod.

1

on business

1

I have a flat.

1

I work in London.

1

We have a son and
a daughter.

1

Where do you work?

1

We are going to Moscow.

1

The work is good.

1

Are you on holiday?

1

Oo vas yes't' n**o**meer? [2]

On nye rab**o**taeet. [2]

Sk**o**l'ka st**o**eet? [2]

S vasm**ee** da deeveet**ee**. [2]

Eta sl**ee**shkam d**o**raga! [2]

Mi khat**ee**m v N**o**vgarat. [2]

Mi khat**ee**m bootirbr**o**di. [2]

Z'dyes' yes't'…? [2]

Gdye kaf**e**? [2]

F kat**o**ram chees**oo**? [2]

Do you have a room? 2

He isn't working. 2

How much is it? 2

From eight until nine. 2

This/It is too expensive! 2

We want to go
to Novgorod. 2

We want some sandwiches. 2

Here there is…? 2

Where is the café? 2

At what time? 2

Seevodnya nam nada dyelat' pakoopkee. [3]

Gdye z'dyes' aftoboos? [3]

Golf neel'zya smatryet'. [3]

Nam nada v bank. [3]

Ya khachu koopeet' foodbolkoo. [3]

Eta fsyo. [3]

Gde z'dyes' magazeen sooveeneeraf? [3]

Magazeeni atkriti da kakova chyasa? [3]

Mi mnoga koopeelee. [3]

Ocheen' doraga stoeet. [3]

Today we must do/
go shopping **3**

Is there a bus here? **3**

It is not possible to
watch golf. **3**

It is necessary for us **3**
(to go) to a bank.

I want to buy a T-shirt. **3**

That/It is all. **3**

Where is there a **3**
souvenir shop?

Shops are open until **3**
what time?

We have bought a lot. **3**

It is very expensive. **3**

Kto-ta pazvan**ee**l.
4

On nye skaz**a**l, pachem**oo**.
4

Oo meen**ya** fstr**ye**chya s neem.
4

Ya yeev**o** zn**a**yu.
4

Tak neel'z**ya**.
4

Shto vi khat**ee**tye peet'?
4

Shto vam?
4

Ocheen' v**a**zhniee d**ee**la.
4

Vi nye m**o**zhitee mnye pam**o**ch'?
4

Kak pa-r**oo**skee...?
4

Someone rang. 4

He didn't say why. 4

I have a meeting with him. 4

I know him. 4

One can't do that. 4

What do you want to drink? 4

What would you like? 4

A very important matter. 4

You couldn't help me, 4
could you?

How do you say... in 4
Russian?

Gdye vagz**a**l?

Kagd**a** atkh**o**deet p**o**eest?

Z'dyes' koor**ee**t' zapreeshsh**a**eetsa.

Da mooz**y**eya daleek**o**?

Z'dyes' yes't' baln**ee**tsa?

Beel**y**etee n**a**da prakampast**ee**ravat'.

Mnye nye nr**a**veetsa...

Taks**ee** nee d**o**raga st**o**eet, patam**oo** shta st**a**roye.

Gdye ma**ya** s**oo**mka?

Ya nad**ye**yus', shto prabl**ye**m nye b**oo**deet.

Where is the station? 5

When does the train leave? 5

It is forbidden to 5
smoke here.

Is it far to the museum? 5

Is there a hospital here? 5

It is necessary to 5
punch (clip) tickets.

I don't like... 5

The taxi is not expensive, 5
because it is old.

Where is my bag? 5

I hope that there won't 5
be any problems.

F paneed**ye**lneek mnye [6]
n**a**da b**oo**deet rab**o**tat'.

Ya nee mag**oo** zhdat'. [6]

Gdye vi zhiv**yo**tee? [6]

Mnye n**a**da koop**ee**t' [6]
s**o**taviiy teeleef**o**n.

Oo nas m**a**leen'kaya [6]
kvart**ee**ra.

Oozh**e** kan**ye**ts [6]
n**a**sheeva **o**tpooska.

Z'dyes' neecheev**o** [6]
patkhad**ya**shsheeva nyet.

V **e**tam gad**oo**... [6]

Kak deel**a**? [6]

D**aiy**tee, pazh**a**loosta, [6]
gaz**ye**too.

On Monday I must work. 6

I can't wait. 6

Where do you live? 6

I must buy a
mobile telephone. 6

We have a small flat. 6

Already it is the end of 6
our holiday.

There's nothing 6
suitable here.

This year… 6

How are you? 6

Please give me the/a 6
newspaper.

This is to certify
that

. . . .

has successfully completed
a six-week course of

Instant Russian

with . . . . results

Date   Instructor